PASSIVE INCOME IN 90 DAYS

How to Passively Make
$1K–$10K a Month in as
Little as 90 Days

William U. Peña, MBA

Contents

Introduction

I want you to imagine living in a land where water is scarce. It is a desert region, with few resources. You live in a small town with many other people, whose only goal in life is to just get by.

One day, one of your neighbors decides to dig a well. All of a sudden, he taps into a water source underground, so that he now has plenty of water to take care of his family for the rest of his life.

You see this and you decide you want a water source of your own, so you begin to dig. You dig, and dig, and dig. But you don't find any water. So you get discouraged and you stop digging.

In a few months, another one of your neighbors digs a well, and she strikes the water source so that she has abundant water for her home and family. You get excited again so you begin to dig again. You dig, and dig, and dig, but still you don't find any water. So you get discouraged and you stop digging.

A few more months later another one of your other neighbors digs a well, and strikes the water source, creating an abundant water supply for his family. You hear about this, but your previous experiences have caused you to doubt that you could ever tap this water source. So this time, you decide not to dig.

As time goes by, more and more of your neighbors dig and strike the water source. But you ignore them, because you say, "It will never happen for me." Or you say, "I tried it but it didn't work."

Then one day, one of your neighbors comes by to visit. And he asks you why you haven't dug your well. You give him every excuse you can think of, "It doesn't work to dig." You say. Or you say, "I've tried digging, but it only works for those other neighbors that are smarter, better, or more experienced than me."

Your neighbor looks at you perplexed, and then he asks you the strangest question, "Didn't you get the map that shows you where the water supply is?" "What map?" You ask. He goes on to tell you that months prior, a representative of the geological society visited the town and gave everyone a map of where the water supply is under their land. It was taken by a radar survey that had been done earlier that year.

Then he shows you the map and you see that the water supply is directly under the entire town. "Then why couldn't I find any water when I dug?" You ask. Your neighbor tells you, "It's because, even though you dug, you stopped digging a few feet before you reached it."

This story illustrates what the pursuit of passive income is like for many people. Many people see the benefits and rewards of passive income. They also believe that financial freedom can produce a great life for them. So they try to build it, but they don't succeed. They try again, and don't succeed. And sometimes they try one more time, and don't succeed. So they give up.

I can relate to this. Personally, I spent 15 years pursuing financial freedom by every means necessary. But every time I tried, I couldn't find it. So, I settled for just being self-employed and trading my time and expertise for money. It wasn't bad, until I stopped working. If I got sick or I took a vacation, then I wouldn't make any money. Obviously, this was not the financially free lifestyle I was looking for.

What was interesting was that the opportunity to build passive income was always there, but I just either did not know how to tap into it, or I quit before I had the chance to find it.

Especially, because in the past, passive income was restricted to investing in real estate or in the stock/ commodities markets. This meant that only the experts were able to do it. And even then, it took a lot of work and a lot of money just to build a few percentages of passive income.

Being the entrepreneur that I was, I just did not have the patience to wait a few years just to make a few extra dollars in passive income every month. So, passive income became a dream. It became something that people would just talk about at parties, but hardly anyone would really achieve. Countless books were written about it, but very few people actually experienced what the authors were talking about. So it became a pipe dream for many, especially me.

Fast-forward to the 21st century, and I found myself again frustrated by the limitations of being self-employed. I finally got sick and tired of trading time for money, so I again decided to make an effort to build passive income.

What I discovered was an absolute shock to me. Where before, there were only a few ways to build passive income, all of a sudden you could find hundreds of ways of creating a stream of income with little effort. Where before, you could only build passive income through investing in real estate, stocks or commodities; now there appeared the idea of starting a passive business that generated passive income with very little work involved.

Where before, only the experts could ever build passive income and you needed lots of money to even start; now, with the latest technology, anyone with a computer, a few dollars and an internet connection could create passive income from the comfort of their own home.

So, with this new environment, and a newfound motivation, I set to work on building passive income. I did the research and committed the time to building enough passive income to replace my current income. I set my goal to be financially free within the next 2 years, because I thought it would take me that long to do it. I focused on three of the easiest passive income streams I could find (which you will learn about later in this book), I crossed my fingers and jumped in with both feet.

Well, I started building passive income in February of 2014, and by September 30th, 2014 I was officially financially free. In just 7 short months I was able to replace my income by 200%, and finally retire from what Robert Kiyosaki endearingly called, the "Rat Race."

This book is my gift to you, to show you that to build passive income, you don't need to be an expert, you don't have to have lots of money, and you don't even need to work very hard at it. You just need to make a commitment to never give up; to keep on digging until you tap into that water source; and to never stop trying until you succeed. Because if you do, success will not be a matter of "If" for you, but only a matter of "When."

CHAPTER 1

Passive Income for Life

Why passive income?
To start, I have a question for you:

"How many hours are you working right now, per week?"

Think about how many hours you put in, day in, day out, either working a full-time job, or being self-employed. Think about how many hours you put in in order to make the money that you need to support your family and take care of the other needs that you have.

The even bigger question is, "Are you okay with that?"

This question really hit me this year. The challenging thing about being a business consultant is that every year you're fighting to get new clients, because at the end of the previous year, all of your clients seem to take off. I've been doing this for about a decade, and this year it finally dawned on me that if I don't work, I don't eat. If I don't work, my family won't eat. Most importantly, this year I realized that this not a place where I want to be.

Do you?

Another question I have for you is:

"Is your lifestyle outpacing your money, or is your money outpacing your lifestyle?"

When you think about inflation and the cost of basic necessities, don't you start to get the feeling that your lifestyle is outpacing your money? Little by little, you have to work twice as hard in order just to make the same amount of money you made the previous year. Now, imagine what it will be like 10 years from now.

So, why passive income? Because passive income helps us escape the employment or self-employment trap, and enter a very special place called financial freedom.

Financial Freedom

And what is financial freedom? Well, financial freedom is when you are generating enough passive income to outpace your current expenses. In other words, you're putting in the least amount of time and effort, but you're making a substantial amount more money, which is taking care of all your financial needs. The best part is, that the income you generate is passive, so that even if you don't work, you still make money.

Now, the type of passive income that leads to financial freedom generally comes from two sources. The first is from automated businesses. Automated businesses are businesses that can run themselves, and still provide you with a substantial income. I call these mini-businesses that take under 10 hours a month to run, but can earn you up to $10K—$20K a month. These are they type of businesses we will be discussing in this book.

The second source of passive income is from passive investments. Passive investments are investments that take little work to manage, but that generate substantial income. Stocks, rental real estate, gold, etc. are examples of investments that can effectively generate great amounts of passive income.

And how do you know when you're truly financially free? When your passive income exceeds your expenses that is when you will be financially free. Meaning, when all the profit that you're generating from your automated businesses or passive investments are exceeding your expenses by at least 150 to 200 percent, then you are completely financially free. The reason, I say 150 to 200 percent is because if any of your passive income streams dry up, you still have enough money coming in that your income will still outpace your expenses.

Benefits of Financial Freedom

Let's now talk about the benefits of being financially free.

1. **Freedom to Build Wealth.** Financial freedom gives you the free time to focus on building wealth. Building wealth, like any important endeavor takes time, and focused effort. If you're busy trying to make ends meet with a job or self-employment, you will never have the time to build wealth for yourself or family. Being financially free changes the game so that you can build the kind of wealth that changes your entire generation.

2. **Freedom to Build Your Health.** With passive income, you don't have to work as hard to support your lifestyle, so you have plenty of time to live a stress-free life that benefits your health.

And, with extra time, you also have time for recreational activities that you think will help you be at your best physical shape.

3. **Freedom to Build Family.** Financial freedom helps your family in a big way by freeing up time that your family deserves. Family was one of my biggest motivations to becoming financially free. I originally went after this because I wanted to help my children grow up with a father in the house, unlike I did. I wanted them to really have me around and so I can be able to develop their characters over time, versus having me at the end of the day when I'm too tired or too worn out to really give to them.

4. **Freedom to Build Your Community.** Being financially free also allows you to build your community. You have a lot more money coming in, so you can contribute more to social causes, as well as give you free time to volunteer at the charity of your choice.

5. **Freedom to Build Your Future.** One of the biggest things that financial freedom provides is present and future stability. This is because you'll have a consistent stream of income that, even though it's controlled by you, it is not dependent on you.

Now, a lot of us know these things, and many of us have already heard a lot about passive income that leads to financial freedom. We've read *Rich Dad, Poor Dad*. We've heard all the infomercials or we've been to countless seminars and workshops. Yet, why is it that we haven't attained financial freedom yet?

Well, some of us just don't know what to do. Maybe there's just so much information out there that we don't know what to do with it.

Others of us know what to do, but don't do what we need to do. Why? Because we become victims of our distractions. The day-to-day work that takes distracts us up all of our time. Or we get isolated, so we unsuccessfully try to attain financial freedom all by ourselves.

And then others of us don't commit to doing what needs to be done. In other words, we know what to do, we start doing it, but then what happens? We give up too early so we don't see the results.

Only when you make the decision to never give up on seeking passive income in your life, will you finally reach it. This has been not only my experience, but the experience of thousands of other people that have reached financial freedom in their lives.

The question I have for you is, "Are you ready to make the commitment to not give up until you finally reach financial freedom in your life?

CHAPTER

2

The Financial Freedom Mindset

I want to get you familiar with something called the Financial Freedom Mindset. The Financial Freedom Mindset is a way of thinking that is focused on creating massive value using the least amount of time, effort, resource, and money. In other words, you are committed to continually creating large income streams but using the least amount of your time and effort to do it.

This is the mindset of the truly successful and financially free entrepreneurs and investors. Their focus is to work very little, create massive value, and use all of their extra time to enjoy the income that comes from their efforts.

A gentleman named Robert Heinlein describes these people really well, when he once said, "Progress isn't made by early risers. It's made by lazy men trying to find easier ways to do something." This is the essence of the Financial Freedom mindset. And in this book, I'm going to be presenting you with a substantial amount of easier ways to generate massive amounts of passive income that will lead to your financial freedom.

The Financial Freedom mindset also leads to the Financially Free Lifestyle. This means living a life where your life comes first, and your work comes second. Too many families and lives have been destroyed because people have chosen to put work first. Not you. You're going to put your life first and find passive ways of making the money you need, to support the lifestyle you want.

In other words, you are going to be working the least amount possible, while making the most money as possible.

Now, you might be thinking, "Wow, that's far-fetched! That can't be true." The fact is, there are thousands of people living this way right now. There is a vast, big world out there full of people that work very little and make substantial amounts of money. Some of them retire in their 50s, 40s, and even 30s. Some are traveling the world; others are devoting their time to serving the world, because they can. So prepare yourself to accept the fact that this opportunity is the reality.

The Financial Freedom Mini-business

Now, in order to build a Financially Free lifestyle, you need the right business to sustain your lifestyle. This is the kind of business that builds, supports, and maintains your passive lifestyle by generating a large monthly income, yet requiring minimum time and effort.

So, what does that look like? Well, it has to be a mini-business, meaning that it generates anywhere between $5,000 and $20,000 per month. Why? Because, if you try to generate more, it generally means more work.

Now, there are ways of generating $1 million dollars a year using very little effort and time, but that's not what this book is about. This book is about how to be become financially free, and for most of us, an extra $5000—$20,000 a month will probably do it for us. And after you become financially free, then you'll have plenty of time to go out and build your millions.

Like we said before, the business must be passive in that you're only working five to ten hours a month, or at most, no more than five to ten hours a week. It's best if it's an automated business, which means that 95% of the work is done for you through the systems, technology and team you use. Also, it should be scalable, meaning that you can grow it in case you decide one day to build a seven-figure income.

The Financial Freedom Plan

Now, in this book we will focus on using what I call the Financial Freedom Plan. The foundation of this path to freedom is that you are going to commit to living out certain principles, week after week after reading this book. And by living by these principles, you will achieve the financial freedom you are looking for.

Here are the commitments your Financial Freedom Plan requires of you:

1. **Choose a passive income goal.**

   Your passive income goal should be approximately 200% of your current expenses. Normally once your passive income exceeds your expenses you are financially free. But you want to set up a cushion for yourself in order to protect yourself in case one of your passive income streams dry up. Also, the extra income will build a healthy reserve that you can further use to build more passive income.

2. **Commit five to ten hours a week toward building passive income streams.**

   What does this mean? This may mean a little bit less TV. This may mean asking the spouse to do a little more, and give you a little extra time for you to focus on financial freedom—especially since it's going to benefit the family. Or, it may mean setting aside five to ten hours over the weekend.

   The main idea is that you are going to dedicate time every week toward building passive income streams for yourself. If you have a job or you are self-employed, you will have to discipline yourself to commit either your nights or weekends to building passive income streams.

3. **Commit to making an additional $100 to $1,000 extra per month in passive income.**

   Every month you will be asking yourself, "How can I make a little bit more passive income this month?" This question will lead you to finding more ways to make an extra $100—$1000 a month in passive income. By doing this every month, before you know it you will be financially free. And no amount is too small. If you make an extra $100 a month in passive income, celebrate. Each passive income dollar you make will eventually lead you to your goal.

4. **Aim to start a new passive income stream every three to six months.**

   The more passive income streams you have, the quicker you will reach your financial freedom goal. Therefore part of the Financial Freedom Plan is to commit yourself to creating a new income stream every three to six months. My speed is pretty fast, so if you're like me you can, create a new passive income stream every month. But on average, to reach your financial freedom goal, you are going to begin a new passive income stream every three to six months.

5. **Commit to Playing the Rich Dad Poor Dad Cash Flow game at least once a week.**

   Robert Kiyosaki's Rich Dad, Poor Dad Cash Flow game is a great training tool to helping you becoming financially free. As of the writing of this book, you can play it online for free. Just go to www.Richdad.com/classic. The goal of the game is to get out of the rat race by building enough passive income to exceed your expenses. It is a great program to keep you focused on getting to your financial freedom goal.

   As a side note, I was able to get to my financial freedom goal within 7 months. I credit the speed that I was able to become financially free to the fact that I played the Cash Flow game three to four times a day, every day, for months.

Expectations

So let's talk more about what you should expect as you embark on your journey toward financial freedom.

1. **It's Going To Take Time.** Expect it to take between three to six months to begin to see results. My path allowed me to begin generating passive income in as little as 30 days. But, generally, expect it to about three to six months. Fight the temptation to get frustrated within the first two weeks if it's not working for you. It's going to take time.

2. **Don't Quit Your Day Job.** It's best to be financially stable when you're building passive income. The reason for this is that it will keep you from being distracted by your own personal financial needs. This way you can have the extra hours to devote to building passive income and not worry about having to make ends meet.

   Now, if you're an entrepreneur, like me, we're generally never financially stable. You're constantly going after one idea, and the next, generating income when luck is in your corner. I wouldn't encourage building passive income in this kind of environment, but don't let that stop you. Who knows, building passive income may create a bit more financial stability for you so you can go out and build the million-dollar company that you're looking to build.

3. **It's Going To Take Commitment.** Like I mentioned before, it is going to mean devoting at least five to ten hours a week to building passive income. Also, you'll need to commit at least

six months to making it work. If in six months it doesn't work, give it up and try something else. I personally don't think you should ever give up, though, because I have personally seen the rewards you receive when you don't give up. And, if it's working for hundreds and thousands of other people, it can definitely work for you, too. So don't give up.

4. **Expect a learning curve.** What I mean by this is that you're going to be testing different ideas, and trying different passive income streams to see if they work for you. Some will work. Some may not. So you will have to be patient with yourself. If it doesn't work the first time, try again. Try it a different way. Keep improving. The idea is that you're constantly learning. But, give yourself the space and patience to learn.

5. **Expect to wait...a lot.** Like I mentioned before, you're going to have to wait. This advice is more for the entrepreneurs like myself, who don't like to wait. There are going to be times where you're going to have to wait to see results. You're going to be throwing out a lot of fishing lines, but you're going to have to wait to catch the fish. This can be difficult, especially if you like to be constantly on the move and if you are addicted to results, like I am. Just, be prepared to wait, or throw out hundreds of fishing lines to speed up the process.

Rewards

Let's now talk about the rewards you can expect from achieving financial freedom:

1. **More Time.** Like we mentioned before, financial freedom will mean more time. If you could imagine for a moment: What would you do if you only had to work ten hours a month? What would you do with all of the extra time on your hands?

   I'll share a quick story about this. Since I started building passive income, I've had very little work to do, and it's been driving, a highly driven entrepreneur like me, crazy. These passive income streams are working so well, that I end up spending my days looking at my email 20 times a day because I've got nothing to do. I'm not kidding you. And I'm not the type to not have anything to do. If there is empty time, I'll create something to do. Yet, since the work is passive, and the income continues to increase, I have to fill the time up with everything else but work.

   It's very similar to when people go on retirement. Most of the time they're not used to their new lifestyle, so they have a really hard time adjusting to it. This is very much what it's like when you become financially free. You're going to be working very little, yet you will still have a lot of money coming in. Psychologically, this is a bit hard for many people to accept. So get ready for it now so that you can be able to live it when it starts happening.

So, be prepared to fill your time with something to do. Since, you will only be work a couple hours a month and still see great financial results.

2. **More Money.** The truth is you're going to have so much money coming in, you're not going to know what to do with it. That's just the way that these passive income streams work. Don't be surprised if you're making $100,000, $250,000 your first year. From my own experience, and after speaking with other financially free individuals, I realized that this is actually the norm.

3. **More opportunities.** More time and more money generally mean more opportunity. This could be more opportunity to build more wealth. Or more opportunity to discover new passive income streams. Or more opportunity to strengthen your relationships. The opportunities are endless.

4. **More contribution.** You'll also have more time to dedicate toward helping others. Your charitable organizations can always use more of your time, as well as more of your financial support. Financial Freedom allows you to do more of both.

5. **More Fun.** And last, you're going to have more fun. More time and more money means more opportunity to travel, to spend time with loved ones, to entertain yourself and others, as well as to do the fun things you love to do.

So strap yourself in, and let's start our journey on toward the path to financial freedom.

CHAPTER
3

Picking the Low Hanging Fruit—Easy Passive Income Ideas

L et's begin by talking about the easiest places you can go to begin building passive income streams.

After doing the research, I can honestly say that there are hundreds of passive business ideas out in the marketplace. In fact, as I was doing my research, there were just so many options that I couldn't keep count. Not only that, but there are thousands of people making money using these ideas.

To give you an idea, here are just a few passive income ideas that require very little money to get started:

1. **Consulting.** If you have knowledge about something that someone else needs then you can easily become a consultant. Consulting doesn't have to mean a lot of work either. My consulting business became passive because I structured it so that I only had to work one day a week, but I was making enough money to take care of my family.

2. **Affiliate marketing.** This is when you market someone else's product and get a percentage of the profits from the sale.

3. **Membership sites.** This involves creating a website where people can pay a monthly fee to learn something, or to be part of a special and exclusive community.

4. **Video training and development sites.** These are sites where people sell video training to students. If you put together a great video, they will sell it for you for a fee.

5. **Search Engine Optimization (SEO).** Businesses still need someone to help their website come up on the first page on search engines (Google, Yahoo, etc.), when potential customers search for their product. With current technology, you can create an SEO company, that manages multiple customer accounts, and only work, at most, five to ten hours a month. All this and you can still make a substantial amount of income for yourself.

6. **Referral Fees.** In today's marketplace you can refer people to a business, and generally be paid a fee for your referral. Even more valuable, is if you refer to a company that bills their customers on a monthly basis. Most of these companies will gladly pay you a monthly referral fee for every month the customer stays with them. So, even though you refer once, you get paid every month for the life of the customer. Web Marketing companies are especially great for this, as well as companies that sell monthly software services.

7. **Book and eBook sales.** Writing eBooks and hardcopy books are a great source of recurring revenue. You write the book

once and it continues to make money for you every month after, with no extra work on your part.

8. **E-commerce.** This includes selling physical products online.

9. **Online product sales.** This includes selling digital information products that like books or eBooks, once created, will continue to sell month after month, without additional effort.

10. **Web design.** If you can outsource the design aspect, then you can take orders online and have your outsource design company do all the work.

From this short list, you can see that there are a substantial amount ways of making passive income.

Now, while reading the list, you may have heard a voice in your head saying, "Oh, well, I'm too old for that," or "That's just too complicated." The truth is that in today's world, there are simplified ways of working every one of these ideas. Or, you can always find somebody else to do the work for you for a low cost. All you would have to do is own the business, outsource the work and collect the checks.

Moderate Passive Income Ideas

If you have capital to invest, you can invest it in multiple passive vehicles that can bring you a healthy return for your investments. Here are just a few.

1. **Rentals.** You can invest in real estate, equipment or services that people want, and then passively rent them out. Passive rental

ideas would include, renting out manufacturing equipment, renting out Port-a-Potties, renting out vending machines, renting out ATM cash machines, etc. Self-service car washes are huge moneymakers. Laundromats are also profitable, especially if they are automated with the latest equipment.

2. **Franchises.** Passive franchises tend to be a bit more expensive, but they generally run themselves and provide substantial passive income. The key is to make sure the franchise requires minimal effort to operate. Frozen yogurt franchises are a good example. All you have to do is find a great company or individual to manage your franchise, and you will automate 95% of the process.

Active to Passive Business Ideas

Active to passive businesses are business where it requires about five years of active work, but if effectively done, will result in producing substantial passive income after. This includes:

1. **Insurance sales.** This is an industry most of us are familiar with. A lot of us know insurance agents that work for a few years, and retire while living off the residual income of their insurance sales.

2. **Network marketing.** The key to success in network marketing is that you work at it for a couple years and then it gives you passive income over time. Once you build an effective network marketing team, you can live off the residual income your team brings you for years to come.

Now, active to passive business are not my cup of tea because I honestly don't want to work actively at all. Also, I like to start making passive income within months not years. But, that's just me. If this is the plan you are currently on, just make sure you have an effective plan, and keep going until you make it.

Passive Income Investments

Investments are normally passive in nature, yet some are more passive than others, and bring higher returns. Here are just a few:

1. **Lending.** This includes peer-to-peer lending, and lending to businesses. Peer-to-peer lending is best done through a service that is experienced in this like Prosper.com or Lending Club. Business lending includes lending money to small businesses that need it for their daily operations. They will pay you a monthly income to use your money. Retail lending is highly lucrative, because there are always retailers looking for loans, especially during holidays and special seasons. And retailers are generally willing to pay higher interest.

2. **Real estate investing.** Now, as you probably know, not all real estate investing is passive. You can spend 80 hours a week trying to make a real estate investment work if you are not careful. On the other hand, there are plenty of passive real estate investments that require little work and provide high monthly income. These include buying rental real estate with a property manager to manage it for you. It also includes wholesaling real estate by buying real estate at a very low price and selling it to a list of hungry investors at a higher price.

3. **Dividend investing.** Dividend investing is investing in stocks that provide a quarterly dividend to their owners. Done effectively, and with a substantial amount of capital to invest, you could create a very stable passive income stream for yourself.

3 Simple and Easy Ways to Make $1K—$10K a Month in Passive Income

The whole purpose of all these lists is to give you an idea of the hundreds of different passive income opportunities that are out in the world today. In this book, though, I am going to focus on three of the simplest ways you can make $1,000 to $10,000 a month in passive income in the next 90 days. These are also the vehicles I used to help me reach my financial freedom goal in just 7 short months.

The strategies I'm going to be teaching you in this book include:

1. **How to make $1,000 to $5,000 a month selling video training products on Udemy.** Udemy is a unique online platform for buying and selling training videos. I'm going to show you the secret to using Udemy to quickly building passive income in as little as 90 days.

2. **How to make $500 to $5,000 a month selling eBooks on Amazon Kindle without doing a lot of writing.** I don't like to work unnecessarily, and that includes writing. Yet, I will show you the simplest way to produce profitable eBooks that customers are hungry for, with very little of your effort.

3. **How to make $1,000 to $10,000 a month selling your own physical products on Amazon.** When people think retail, they think

they have to work a lot and carry a lot of inventory. In this book I will show you the simplest way to sell abundant physical products on Amazon while automating 95% of your work. The best part is that you won't have to carry any inventory.

The Passive Income Success System

In order to be successful at the strategies we will cover in this book, as well as any other passive income business you start, you will need to approach it using, what I call, The Passive Income Success System. This success system is designed to help you achieve success with every passive income stream you start. It has worked in helping me generate $15K—$20K in passive income in 7 months, and it continues to work in any new passive income businesses I start.

So what is the Passive Income Success System? The Passive Income Success System is a business model that is designed to work in creating the most passive income, in the shortest amount of time. The best part is that you can apply it to any passive income situation or strategy.

Here are the main parts to the Passive Income Success System:

1. **Identify successful passive income streams that are working for other people.**

   To start, you should pick a passive income stream that has been proven to work for many other people. This is not the place to come up with new ideas the world hasn't seen yet. You can do that later when you are financially free. Here we want to find the ideas that have made hundreds of other people financially free, so that it can work for you too.

2. **Find the best practices that will achieve the most success for that passive income stream.**

This will take a little research on your part, but if done well, it is totally worth it. The goal is to identify the best practices and most effective system that other successful people have used in a particular industry to build their passive income. The little time you put in researching the best practices, the quicker you will get to your financial freedom goal.

Generally, you can find all of the information you need on the Internet or in books written by highly successful passive income entrepreneurs.

3. **Test and validate on a small scale until you make it work for you.**

Even though you will be following the "best practice," you will still need to test and verify that it will work for you. This means taking time to test and tweak your efforts until you make it work for you or you discover it is not a good fit for you.

4. **Automate the process.**

Once you get the system working for you, then you automate the process until you're working only ten hours a month, maximum. The idea is to build passive income, not just income. There must be an effort at using systems, technology, a team, and outsourcing in order to reduce the time, effort, resources and money you use to produce your income.

5. **Scale the system until you're making as much money as you want.**

The last step is to continue to grow and expand the business, until you are making as much money as you want. Just remember to keep testing and tweaking in order to maintain your work hours to only 10 hours a month, max. If you do it effectively enough you could even be making 7 figures putting in very little time and effort.

So, now let's jump into learning about the first simple way to make $1,000 to $5,000 a month in passive income.

PART 1

Passive Income Idea #1: Udemy

Now, I know that Udemy may be new to a lot of people, so I want to start by getting you acquainted with this giant in the video training sales business.

So, what is Udemy? Udemy (You—Demy vs. Academy) is a self-education website, that provides people from around the world, the opportunity to learn everything from simple to highly advanced subjects. Udemy hosts about 20,000 courses ranging from free up to $499 per course. It also provides a wide range of courses to fit every need. The courses are mostly presented via video, but they also include training manuals, and eBooks as well.

Udemy is also a great way for coaches, trainers or professionals to promote video content that they've created, and bring it to the public. Udemy provides a user-friendly video training-hosting platform that provides all of the resources an instructor needs to upload, promote and sell different types of video training courses. The best part of all, is that it gives instructors access to a ready-made audience full of millions of students that are eager to learn and buy their videos.

I came across Udemy in early February or March of the year I wrote this book, and in three to four months I started making between $2,000 to $5,000 a month selling my video courses on Udemy. What I was most pleased and surprised about was, how amazingly quick and easy it is to make money from this place.

So, in this section I want to talk about the secrets to successfully selling video courses on Udemy. In fact, if you follow this system you are about to learn, you will be able to make you an extra $1,000 to $5,000 per month selling video courses on Udemy.

Like I mentioned previously, don't listen to the voices in your head that are telling you, "Oh, I don't know how to make a video course," or "That just seems so foreign to me," etc. The truth is that I spend at most, three to four hours a month doing it, and I'm making thousands of dollars in passive income every month doing this. I cannot stress enough how very simple selling on Udemy really is.

To start, if you don't know Udemy, take a quick glimpse at the Udemy website, at http://www.Udemy.com.

The Udemy Selling Success System

Now, let's dive into the best practices for successfully selling video courses on Udemy. Here is a quick overview:

1. **Pick The Most Desirable Topics.** In other words, finding the subjects that people are very eager to learn, and eager to purchase.

2. **Create Valuable And Interesting Courses.** Make your video courses so valuable to your students that you not only make a lot of sales, but you become highly popular with the entire Udemy community.

3. **Build Your List of Hungry Students.** Udemy makes it possible to build your own personal list of students that you can communicate with over time. The goal then is to build your student base so big that promoting your video courses to them becomes a breeze.

4. **Effectively Promote Your Courses To Your Students.** Learn the multiple ways to best promote your video courses to make the most profit.

5. **Grow Your Udemy Business and Increase Your Income.** Use different opportunities in Udemy to grow your business even bigger and increase your income even larger.

And just to give you a quick idea of how passive Udemy is, I literally only send out two to four emails a month, and I make about $2,000 to $5,000 a month in passive income every month. This how dialed in this Udemy Success System is.

At most, you can expect to spend anywhere from five to ten hours a month and make anywhere from $1,000 to $5,000 a month, and sometimes more. In fact, as of the writing of this book, the top 10 Udemy instructors combined have made close to $2 Million dollars in profit for themselves.

Rewards of Selling on Udemy

So what benefits and rewards can you expect from selling video courses on Udemy?

1. **You can make $1,000 to $5,000 or more every month, working less than ten hours a month.** You make enough extra money, to either add to your current income, or even replace it.

2. **You get to see results quickly.** You can make a video today, upload it to Udemy today, and begin building your student list today. Within a month you will have thousands of students that you can promote a more advanced paid course to, and start making money.

3. **You can share your message with the world.** If you have a message that is on your heart, that you want to share with the world, Udemy gives you a great opportunity to do so. Since Udemy has students from all around the world, you can promote your message to a global audience of millions of people, and get your message out to as many people as possible.

CHAPTER 4

Picking Desirable Video Course Topics

So, how does one pick the most desirable topics for videos that people will want to buy?

The initial temptation will be to create a video course of a subject that you are familiar with. Now, you may be great at a business, or an industry or have some advanced skill. You may even have a great idea that you want to get out to the world. And although this may seem like the easiest and most practical approach for picking a topic, it is generally not the most effective.

What you will find, is that even though you do all the work to put a video course together, it does not mean that anyone will want your video. Why? Because people are only going to buy what they want. So the smart approach is to first find out what people want, and then give it to them.

Creating a great video that nobody wants will quickly put you in the poor house. On the other hand, identifying what people want, and then giving it to them will grow your passive income with amazing speed. Not to mention it makes the entire process a whole lot easier.

Here are two of the most effective ways to uncover popular topics in Udemy:

Using the Udemy Search Filter To Find Hot Topics

The first step finding popular topics is to use Udemy's database to find out what the most popular topics are. Udemy makes it very easy by giving you an option to filter your search results by Popularity, Reviews, Number of Students, etc.. Once you filter your results, and see what videos are in greatest demand, then you can begin to consider what video topic you will choose.

1. **Searching by Popularity**—Udemy's Popularity filter will show you the most popular topics in each Course Category. It determines a course's popularity by the most student sign ups within a certain period (probably 30 days). It is the best source for information about hot topics because it is the most recent and accurate.

2. **Searching by Number of Students.** Just like the Udemy search filter for Popularity, the filter for Number of Students can also give you great insights as to the topics that have been engaged by the most students in Udemy.

Now you may be wondering what's the difference between the "Popularity" filter and the "Number of Students" filter. Well, the Popularity filter is based on the most recent amount of signups in a course (most likely in a 30 day period). The Number of

Students filter gives you the amount of students that have registered in a course for the life of the course program.

Even though Popularity is the better gauge for a hot topic, the Number of Students filter will give you an overall history so that you can see the trends as to what the most popular topics historically have been.

3. **Searching by Reviews.** The best reason to search by reviews is because, if a course has a lot of reviews, it usually means that the course has attracted the most active students. So whatever topic these active students are attracted to, it's a good chance that if you create a similar topic it will attract similar students.

Also, if the students give a video course great reviews, it shows that the course was of very high quality. This gives you a great resource, which you can use as a template for when you design your courses.

Last, the more reviews you get, and the more sales you attract. So if you create similar courses to courses with a lot of great reviews, then you can generally expect a lot more sales as well.

The Udemy Hot Topic Filtering Process

Here is the system that I use in order to identify the hottest topics, filter out the not so hot topics, and to show me which topics will help me make money right away:

1. Click on Udemy's Browse Courses button (Usually on the upper left side of screen).

2. When the list of course categories comes up, click on the general Course Category you are Interested in doing a course in.

3. Click on the Udemy filter dropdown box and choose Popularity, Number of Students, Reviews, Price, etc. (usually on right side of screen).

4. Go through the list of video courses to see if you can find a paid course topic that describes a subject you are good at, or you have some familiarity with.

5. If you do not find a subject that you are familiar with, go to another general Course Category and go through the process over again.

Getting Help from the Udemy Staff

Udemy also has an incredibly supportive staff. The reason for this is because Udemy knows that if you make money, then they make money (as of this writing it is a 50/50 profit share split). Therefore, they are a great resource for asking advice on the kind of topics that their Udemy students are looking for, and they're incredibly supportive in helping you market your videos too.

The Udemy staff also has a better perspective on topics that sell, the topics that are most popular, topics that are in high demand, etc. This is because all of the data is at their fingertips, and they need to know it to promote the best courses to make money. It is like having your own market research team at your disposal.

Now, the best way to get help from the Udemy staff is to reach out to the person, which sends you an introduction email when you first create an Udemy account. Don't just ask them to give you the next hot topic, though. You need to make their job easier, by having a list of different topics that you've researched and then ask them which they think would be best to start with. Remember, they want you to succeed because if you make money, they make money.

CHAPTER

5

Creating Valuable and Interesting Video Courses

The next step to successfully selling video courses on Udemy is to make your Udemy courses really valuable and really interesting. The best part of this is that the Udemy community of students are a great bunch to work with, and easy to please.

Udemy students are generally looking for great, valuable, and actionable content that works. So the first thing I do is to make sure that the content I want to put out really brings results. The only content I put in my courses is information that I have proven to work for me, or that I have verified that it has been proven to work for people I know that are credible. The more valuable, actionable, content that works you provide, the greater the amount of people that will want to buy your course.

Another great benefit that Udemy students look for is a user-friendly layout of your course that flows. If you make your courses easy to follow, and easy to understand, people will feel at ease learning from you. I tend to follow the same format for all my video courses so students know what to expect. And they really appreciate it too.

Here is the format that I use in most of my Udemy videos, that seems to be very popular with the Udemy community:

1. **Introduction and Overview of Entire Course (5—15 minutes)**

   a. Introduction—Who I am and my credentials.

   b. Overview—All the main topics we will cover in the course

2. **Expectations and Rewards (5—15 minutes)**

   a. Expectations—What they need to expect in terms of the results they can get from content.

   b. Rewards—The rewards they can expect from putting to practice the content of the course.

3. **Background Information that is Required for Course (5—15 minutes)**

   a. In case you are introducing a topic that is new to the student, they'll need background to facilitate learning.

4. **Topic Points (I usually have anywhere from 5—10 Topic Points) (5—15 minutes each)**

   a. Sub point (3—5 sub points)

   b. Sub-Sub point (3—5 sub-sub points)

   c. Step by Step Process (I only add this on the paid courses)

5. **Conclusion—Recap of all Topic Points (Reuse Overview) (5 minutes)**

6. Action Plan (Usually only on paid courses)
   (Either text or Downloadable)

7. Resources and Bonuses (Either text or Downloadable).

Another component that Udemy students really like, and that makes your video course really great, are all of the extra resources you provide. This includes downloadable templates, checklists, links to more resources, articles, etc. The more resources you add, the more valuable the video course becomes, which will allow you to charge a higher price, that Udemy students will gladly pay for.

Bonuses are a great addition, because they also add value to your course. You can provide links to downloadable content that you create. Or you can provide them discounts to your other courses. I have a link to the EBook companion to my video course that brings me a lot more traffic to purchase my EBook. The student feels happy because they just obtained another resources that will help them succeed.

The Easiest Way to Create a Kick Butt Video Course

By far the greatest source for ideas on making really valuable Udemy courses is to look at what your successful competitors are doing. That's what I do. I always look at who the most successful competitors are in different categories, and I make sure to find out what they're doing. There is good chance that if you imitate the successful people that make money, then you will make money.

In order to get access to video courses of successful Udemy sellers, it usually means having to purchase their courses, which range from $29—$499. In order to bypass spending this kind of money on research, I will either 1) Check out the preview intro video that they post for free on their Udemy course listing (this usually gives me an idea of what to expect in the rest of the course); or 2) Check out the Free Preview of their course promoted by Udemy on search engines. This official free preview you can find by searching for the course on Google. When you click on the link, you get access to entire course for 5 minutes, which is plenty of time to do the research that you need.

Another strategy I use to optimize my video courses is to get a lot of feedback from my students as well. Once I upload a video and students begin to sign up, I'll message them through Udemy and ask them, "Hey, is this working for you? Or, "Do you like this course?" and, "What do you like most about it?" Usually they'll tell me and I take their suggestions and improve the course. Next thing you know, you get more and more people registering for your video course.

CHAPTER

6

Building Your List of Hungry Student Buyers—The Holy Grail in Udemy

The Holy Grail for success in Udemy is building your list of hungry student buyers. If you've ever tried to build an email list out on Internet, you know how incredibly challenging it is to do. But, having a huge email list of people interested in what you are offering is the key to success in Internet marketing. If you have a list of hungry buyers, then you have the opportunity to constantly promote your new products to them.

The great thing about Udemy is that Udemy makes it the easiest thing in the world to build a massive list of hungry student. And the more students you have in your classes, the more you can promote your paid courses to them. You see, Udemy allows you to message your students about new courses that you're putting out. So you can continue to promote old and new paid courses to your student list, month after month, or until the cows come home. This is the foundation of your entire Udemy Success System.

In just six short months, I was able to get 20,000 unique students. Imagine, in about six short months I was able to do what would generally take two years to do on the Internet. My ultimate goal is to get 100,000 to 200,000 students. Why? Because then I can continuously promote the new courses that I come out with. I can promote my $99—$199 courses and a lot of students will buy them. And, when I promote my video courses by offering discounts, people feel like it's a great opportunity, and they'll jump at the chance at buying my courses.

So, how does one build a list of hungry students on Udemy so quickly? The key is offering a lot of free stuff. You see, just like on the Internet, Udemy students are looking for a lot of free courses. So, what I do is create anywhere from 5—10 video courses and offer them for free on Udemy. They will be high quality video courses that range from 45 minutes to an hour.

Once students find my videos (thanks to Udemy's aggressive marketing campaigns) they begin to sign up right away. Using this strategy, I generally get 100—300 students signing up for my free courses every day. Before long I have 1000 students that I can message directly; and eventually 10,000 or 20,000.

The next step is to run promotions to those students, for all my paid courses. By offering a discount, students jump at the chance at buying them at such a great deal. The reason they are so eager is that since they already find a lot of value in my free courses, they are really eager to buy my paid courses. At the normal price, these paid courses are a bit expensive for them. Once I run my promotion (usually for 3—5 days), they jump at the opportunity to learn more from me.

It's Internet marketing 101. Yet, within Udemy, building a list of hungry students to promote your video courses to feels like the easiest thing in the world.

CHAPTER 7

Promoting Your Courses for Massive Sales

So how do you promote your courses? First, it's good to know that with Udemy, the majority of your sales will be made through promotions. In other words, the Udemy community is trained to purchase video courses through the many promotions course authors offer every month. So, be prepared to be constantly promoting.

For example, though I will price a video course at $199, most of my sales come from promotions. I'll promote that course different times of the month for $49, $29, or even for $19. And people will keep on buying as long as you offer them great promotions.

Now, the best part is that not only will you be promoting your video courses, but Udemy will also be actively promoting your courses as well. Remember, Udemy knows that if you make money, they make money. So they have created a very effective marketing department that promotes video courses to their student community, throughout the Internet, and through social media as well.

Udemy students are highly motivated to buy for a few reasons. The first is scarcity. If you can announce time limits on your promotions, such as "Only three days left." It creates enough scarcity that will motivate buyers to purchase out of fear of losing the deal. They're also motivated by opportunity. The kind of opportunity you find when you make an offer like, "$199 for only $19!" Or "90 percent Off On All of Our Most Popular Courses!" Last, they are motivated to buy from you if they like you. Meaning, if they liked your other free or paid videos, they'll keep on buying any new video courses you come out with.

Again, it is just marketing 101, but Udemy makes it really easy to do.

CHAPTER

8

Growing Your Udemy Selling Business and Grow Your Income

A nother great opportunity you can find in Udemy is in how easy it is to grow your Udemy business and increase your income.

For example, if you have 10,000—20,000 unique registered students in your courses, every paid course should bring you anywhere from $500 to $1,000 a month. If you decide to create a course every month, by the end of six months, you will have 6 paid courses. This will bring you anywhere from $3,000 to $6,000 a month in income.

Can you begin to understand how much money you can make using this Udemy Selling System?

And this is not theory. I'm actually doing this right now. I'm putting out two courses a month and I'm literally getting anywhere from $500 to $1,000 a month per course, so you imagine how much money I'm making right now.

My goal is to add two paid courses every one to two months. But, you can also do one every three to six months, if that is more convenient for you. Just remember to keep adding free courses, because that's how you get more and more students to sign up on your list.

Also, try selling video courses in different categories. For example, most of my video courses are in the category of business. Yet, I also added a motivation course in a completely different category. By doing this I've created multiple ways I can make money from different audiences.

Udemy Recap and Resources

In conclusion, how do you make money selling video courses on Udemy? By picking desirable topics students love; by creating valuable and interesting courses; building your list of hungry students; effectively promoting your courses to those students; and then scaling and growing your Udemy business, to grow your monthly passive income.

Now, if you would like a more detailed, step-by-step training on making money selling video courses on Udemy, then click on the link below and sign up for my Udemy video course titled: "How to Make $1K—$5K Selling Video Courses on Udemy," which you can find at this link.

www.udemy.com/create-passive-income-successfully-selling-courses-on-udemy/

Normally it retails for $149, but as a bonus for reading this book, you can get the course for $49 by using the coupon code: PENAPROMO49.

Now let's look at another simple, yet effective way to make another $500—$5000 a month in passive income, so you can get even closer to reaching your financial freedom goal.

PART 2

Passive Income Idea #2: Kindle

call our next opportunity, "Kindle Selling Secrets; How to make $500 to $5,000 Selling EBooks on Kindle."

Now if you're like me, you may think, "Oh, great. Does this mean I have to write a book? That's as easy as climbing a mountain." But please trust me when I tell you, there are great ways, which I'm going to show you, to write a book without picking up a pen or tapping a key on your computer.

Let's begin by discussing an overview of the best practices of selling eBooks on Kindle. Here are a few things we are going to discuss in this section.

1. **Picking a hot subject for your e-book.** This is the foundation of your Kindle eBook business and we will look at some of the quickest ways to find the hottest subjects to write eBooks about.

2. **Test and validate your eBook.** You want to make sure that before you put the time and effort into actually writing your eBook, you need to find out if people even want to buy it.

3. **Passively produce your eBook.** In order to create passive income streams, it means working as little as possible, but make as much money as possible. We will look at how to produce your eBook with doing very little writing.

4. **Get great reviews for your eBook.** Reviews are the Holy Grail in Amazon Kindle, because the more great reviews you get the more sales you will make.

5. **Pricing and promoting your eBook for maximum sales.** Learn how to choose the best pricing to get the most amount of customers to buy from you. Also, once you write your book, how do you

get it to the public? We are going to look at ways to quickly get your eBook to as many people as possible.

6. **Grow your Kindle eBook business, and grow your income.** Once you master the system, there is a great opportunity to grow your Kindle eBook business, and increase your passive income month per month.

Rewards of Selling Kindle EBooks

Now, what are the rewards of starting a Kindle eBook business? For starters, you can make $500 to $5,000 a month without much extra work. This is currently the norm for successful eBook sellers on Kindle. A second reward is that, it only takes two to five hours a week to produce your eBook. And, if you do it right, it generally takes even less than that. Once you produce your eBook, your work is done, and that one eBook will sell over and over again, making you money, even while you sleep.

Last, and the part I love the most, there are many ways, to produce your Kindle eBook with very little writing. This means you can produce as many eBooks as you want and grow your passive income to whatever level you need, and still only work a few hours a month.

CHAPTER

9

Picking a Hot Topic for Your EBook

So how does one pick the hottest topics that will motivate people to spend money to buy your Kindle eBook? First you need to set up the right criteria that will help you find the hottest topics in the Amazon Kindle marketplace. Here are the criteria I use when I am looking for the next topic for my eBook.

The Amazon Kindle Bestseller List

When I am doing research for a hot topic, the first place I go is the Amazon Kindle Bestseller Kindle list. Here, it shows you exactly what the most popular topics are, if you know how to look. Now, when you first visit the Bestseller list you can get lost among all the titles. But the following criteria gives a way to filter out the best topics that will more guarantee the success of your next eBook.

1. **Non-Fiction**—Non-fiction books are the simplest to produce, as well as there is more of a guarantee that they will make money.

This is because, with non-fiction books, people can see more of a concrete return in terms of a problem solved. Also, non-fiction far outpaces fiction books on Kindle, so the lion's share of business will go to those that produce non-fiction eBooks.

If you're into fiction, you may have to wait till you're financially free to write the next great American novel. But, for now, if you want to make money, stick to non-fiction.

2. **Sales Rank**—When I am doing research on the Amazon Bestseller list, the first thing that I do when I am looking for a topic that I am interested in, is look at the book's sales rank. The sales rank is Amazon's way of telling the public which book is selling most. The book that is at number one in sales rank, is the highest selling eBook in Kindle, and is selling about 4000+ books a day. On the contrary, the book with a sales rank of 10,000 sells about 15 books a day. Below is a quick look at sales rank and how many books need to be sold to reach that rank:

   - Rank 50,000 to 100,000—selling 0—1 book a day.
   - **Rank 10,000 to 50,000—selling 3 to 15 books a day.**
   - **Rank 5,500 to 10,000—selling 15 to 30 books a day.**
   - Rank 3,000 to 5,500—selling 30 to 50 books a day.
   - Rank 500 to 3,000—selling 50 to 200 books a day.
   - Rank 350 to 500—selling 200 to 300 books a day.
   - Rank 100 to 350—selling 300 to 500 books a day.
   - Rank 35 to 100—selling 500 to 1,000 books a day.
   - Rank 10 to 35—selling 1,000 to 2,000 books a day.

- Rank of 5 to 10—selling 2,000 to 4,000 books a day.
- Rank of 1 to 5—selling 4,000+ books a day.

When I am doing research in the Amazon Kindle Bestseller list, I want to find the books that have a sales rank between 5,000—30,000. This is what I call the Kindle sales sweet spot. Why? Because I know that if I pick a topic similar to books that sell at this ranking, I can do equally well. Also, it is also the range that gives me competition that is not too difficult to beat. Also, my target profit is $500—$1000 a month per eBook, and this gives me enough sales to reach my goal.

If I find a topic that fits within this sales rank, I will do research on this topic to see if there are any more titles that fall within this sales rank as well. You see, if one book ranks well in my topic, it may be a fluke. But if you have three or four that are also ranking in this range, then there is a good chance that there is a big market for this topic.

3. **Competition**—After doing the research above, I then search for how strong the competition is for my particular topic. When I do a search for the topic, if I notice that I am up against some big name authors with huge followings, or even celebrities, I will not try to compete. Why? Because I want to be the big fish in the small pond. Once I get big enough, I may move ponds. But when doing my research I stay away from the heavy competition.

Next, I look at how many authors have written about my topic. I try to look for topics with under 30 authors in the topic. This shows me I have a great chance at becoming a bestseller in this category. On the other hand, if a topic has thousands of authors, then my chances of becoming a bestseller are slim.

Now I will add an exception to this. If you write a very valuable and amazing book, it doesn't matter what the competition is. You can still become a bestseller in this category among hundreds of authors competing against you. But, remember, it doesn't matter if you think your book is valuable and amazing. It only matters if the buyer does.

Hot Niches on Amazon Kindle

Now, there are some topics that naturally have huge audiences. Below is a list of some naturally hot subject niches that you could write about and generally make a lot of sales from:

Health
- Avoiding Stress
- Natural Weight Loss/ Fat Loss
- Getting Ripped/Gaining muscle
- Easy and Low Impact Exercises
- Organic and Raw Food
- Holistic Medicine Alternatives
- Very Specific Health Problems.
  - I.e. Food Allergies

Love and Dating

- How to attract opposite sex
- Sex
- Dating
- Maintaining Relationships
- Marriage
- Conflict Resolution
- Parenting and Education
- Body Language

Business and Money

- Investing (Stocks, etc.)
- Foreign Exchange Trading
- Retirement
- Debt
- Making Money Online
- Starting a specific business
- Real Estate/Real Estate Investing
- Marketing and Internet Marketing
- Productivity and Time Management
- Getting Hired

Hobby Niches:

- Home and Garden
- Arts and Entertainment

- Travel

- Pets

Recreation:
- Sports

- Boating/Running/ Hiking

For example, let's say you go to the Amazon Kindle Bestseller list in the health category. All of a sudden you find a book about lemon recipes on the bestseller list. You check out the book and see that it's sales rank is 10,000, which is within our sales rank range. You do a further check and you see that there are only 20 people that have written about it. This would be a great opportunity for a hot topic that you can write your next eBook about and cash in on.

Now, I know what you're thinking. "I don't know anything about lemon recipes." My answer is, "Who cares?" That is not the point. The point is that you found a market for something that people want. All we need to do is produce the book that's going to fulfill that need. In other words, once you find the market, the actual book, as you will see later, is very simple to produce.

Finding Hot Topics Through Keyword Research

Another way to find hot topics to write about is by using Keyword Research software. Keyword Research software are programs that are designed to show how many people have searched a particular keyword on the Internet or in Amazon itself. A good example of this is the Google Adwords Google Keyword Planner. You can add a keyword of a topic you are interested in writing about and it will let you know how many people are actually searching for the term on Google.

When I use this method, I look for keywords that have a search volume of 50,000 or more. This level of volume tells me that there are enough people looking for that keyword, that there is a good chance that there will be a market for a book I write.

Two other software you can use, that are more focused on Amazon searches only, are FreshKey and MerchantWords. This software will give you the most popular terms that buyers are looking for when they do searches specifically in Amazon. Although they are paid services, I prefer using these instead of the Google Keyword Planner since they provide the search volume and customer patterns that pertain only to Amazon.

Once I know that a search term is popular in Amazon, I will then do my research of the topic using all the criteria I mentioned before. Using this process has allowed me to create two titles that have consistently hit the number one ranking in each of their categories. The result is that it has brought me a consistent passive income month after month.

CHAPTER
10

Guaranteeing Your Kindle EBook's Success

Now, let's talk about how to guarantee your Kindle eBook's success. One of the best ways to guarantee that you'll be able to make a lot of sales from your Kindle eBook, is to make sure that people are going to buy your book, even before you write your book. I am talking about testing and validating your eBook before you actually produce it.

The way that I test and prove that there is a market for my book, is by preselling my book before I produce it. I do this by creating a book cover, and putting it out to the Amazon market, and see if anybody buys it. The reason I do this is that I don't want to spend the effort, the time, or even pay somebody to write the book, when I don't know if people even want it yet.

What I have found is that the best way to confirm if people want your book is with cold hard cash. In other words, if customers buy your book on a pre-sale, even before you have produced it, it means that they value it so much that they will spend money on just the idea of one day owning your book. If 25, 50 or even 100 people do this, you will have confirmed that you have a very hot book on your hands.

How to Test Your EBook Before You Do Any Writing Using Amazon Advantage

Here is the process that I follow to make sure there is a market for my book before I write it:

1. **Get an EBook Cover Made**—First thing I do is I go to Fiverr. com and find a graphic designer to design an eBook cover for me. If you don't know Fiverr.com, it's a place where you can get a lot of great things done, whether graphics or other small business resources, for five dollars or a little bit more. The graphic artist I use on Fiverr.com, does all of my eBooks and I only spend $5 for each one. She is great woman, and she's excellent at what she does.

2. **Get an ISBN Number**—The next step is that I go to Amazon CreateSpace to get a free ISBN number that I will use later for marketing my book. If you do not know CreateSpace, it is Amazon's publishing company, that is one of the most user-friendly ways to publish a paperback book online. They also provide a free ISBN number, which we will need for the next step of the process.

   Since I am only going to CreateSpace to get an ISBN number, I will usually begin the process as if I was publishing an actual paperback book. I will fill out the form, until I get to the section for choosing an ISBN. I will get my ISBN number, and then I will put the application on hold, since I am not actually going to publish a paperback book at that time.

3. **Pre-sell Your Book**—Then I go to Amazon Advantage. Amazon Advantage is another department in Amazon where you can sell items (usually books) on consignment. Once you sign up for an Amazon Advantage account, then you upload your book information. You choose a sale date that is 4—8 weeks in the future and then you publish your book. Your book will then go live in 15—30 minutes, which begins your pre-selling stage of your book.

4. **Wait a Few Weeks to Confirm Your Results**—Give yourself between 4—8 weeks to see if there is a market for your book. If only a few people have bought your book within that time, then it's better to find another topic and book and start from scratch. If 25—50 people pre-order your book, then it probably means you have a winner on your hands.

As a side note, many people have asked me what to do about the paperback orders that they get from using this method, since they are only putting out a Kindle eBook. My answer is if you sell 25—50 copies, and have proven you have a hot topic, make your eBook, and then put the time and money into making a paperback. You've already proven that people want the paperback book, so you might as well make money from that too. If you don't get 25 orders, then after 8 weeks, just cancel the title. Amazon will go ahead and cancel the few orders customers placed, for you.

By following the process above, when I launched my first eBook, I pre-sold 400 copies of the book, even before I produced it. That gave me the confidence to go and produce the eBook. Once I published my eBook, it became number one in its category on the best-seller list for multiple weeks.

CHAPTER 11

Passively Produce Your EBook with Very Little Writing

By now, you may be thinking, "Okay, Will, you got me interested. Now I feel a little better about actually making the effort for this. But I still have to produce the eBook, don't I?"

Well, I want to show you how to passively produce your eBook, with a lot less effort and a lot less writing than you may think.

So, how do you passively produce an eBook? Well, there are three main ways to do this.

1. Record Your EBook and Transcribing It
2. Hiring a Ghostwriter or Researcher.
3. Partnering Up With Someone.

Record Your EBook and Transcribing It

In the previous section of this book we spoke about recording video courses on Udemy. Well, did you know you can take your video courses and hire a professional transcriptionist to transcribe your entire course? Once transcribed you can clean it up and publish it on Kindle. This is how I write most of my books.

There are many benefits from approaching your writing this way, including:

1. **Very Little Researching and Writing**—Because your video courses are full of all the content you need, there is little need to do research or to write down what you need to say. The transcribed document of your recording will generally contain all of the information that you need to put in your book to give value to your readers.

2. **Very Little Editing**—Professional transcribers are 98% accurate with their transcriptions of your recording. This means that your editing will be minimal. You will probably only edit the book to be more user-friendly to a reader, to adapt the content to an eBook format, and to help the book flow better.

3. **Very Little Time Producing**—By using this method, my eBooks take between 2—4 weeks to produce and publish on Kindle. Compare that to the 6—12 months most people spend on writing an eBook that they may not even publish.

4. **More Guarantee that Your eBook Will be Successful**—By transcribing your Udemy video courses, you can get a good idea if there is a demand for your topic by the response you get from

your Udemy audience. If you have thousands of students signing up for your Udemy course, who also give it great reviews, then there is a good chance that your eBook will have great success on Kindle, as well.

Now, you may be thinking that your transcribed Udemy video course may not be long enough to create a standard eBook on Kindle. From my experience, I find that when I have my Udemy course transcribed, I usually end up with more than enough content for a good eBook. You see, when it is converted to a Kindle Book, it produces about double the amount of pages. So you will usually have about 50—100 pages of content for your eBook, which is plenty.

Now, if you have not recorded any video courses on Udemy, you can still use this method to reduce the amount of time and effort it takes to write an eBook. You do this by recording your book on an audio recorder, which can send to a transcriptionist to transcribe. Similar to the previous strategy of recording video courses on Udemy, you can record one to two hours of content and end up with 50 to 100 pages of content for your eBook.

Just a side note, as of the writing of this book, this is the preferred method for many celebrities that write their own books. They simply speak their book into a recorder, send it to a transcriptionist to transcribe, and then send it to an editor to produce the final book. So, if they can do it, why can't you?

Hire a Ghost Writer or Researcher

In today's market, there are really great writers that sell their writing services, which makes them a great resources for writing your eBook. You can hire a "ghostwriter" as they call themselves, for a small hourly fee. They can do the research and write your eBook for you. You just need to provide them with the topic.

Why would writers do this? Because some writers are not interested in writing a bestselling eBook. They are just glad to make extra money doing what they love to do.

You can find great ghostwriters on Elance.com, Odesk.com or Fiverr.com. These are websites that give you access to hundreds of writers that will do all kinds of writing for you for a fee. All you have to do is post a job, and then interested writers will apply for the job. Once you check all of the applications for you post, you pick the one you like.

The best ghostwriters are those that already familiar with your topic. Since they know the topic, they have already done the research, and can quickly and easily put together a 30—50 page paper on the subject. Just make sure it is original content, and that once they sell it to you, it becomes yours, meaning there will be no duplicate copies of the material sold to anyone else.

Once you choose a ghostwriter you can work with, you just give them the topic, the criteria you are looking for in your eBook, and how many pages you want it. Since each 8 ½ by 11" page of content equals about two pages of Kindle eBook content, then you can get affordably pay for 20—30 pages of content, which you can turn into a full length eBook.

You can even ask them to format your eBook according the criteria you learned in this book, including a table of contents, resources, bonuses, etc.

Now, if you don't mind doing the writing yourself, you can hire a researcher to research your topic in order to find great content for your eBook. A researcher is similar to ghostwriter, in that you can contract their services to do research for your next eBook. The only difference is that, instead of writing, they will just give you the raw data, or the summary of the data they have researched for a fee.

Since researchers only do research, they are generally less expensive than ghostwriters. And you can usually find researchers that are experts in a particular topic, which allows them to provide the information you need quickly and affordably.

Last, one of the greatest benefits of using a ghostwriter is that if you find a great one, they can write multiple eBooks for you in a variety of topics. You can churn out 5—10 bestselling eBooks in a year, doing very little or any writing at all.

Partnering Up

Another popular method to produce an eBook, is to partner up with someone you know that is a writer or that loves to write. Most people have a friend, family member or associate that enjoys writing on their spare time. You can easily partner with this person as a co-author for your eBooks.

You can both use your strengths and churn out eBooks every few months. You can do the research and your partner does the writing. Or you can both do research and writing on different parts of the topic. Or, you can be responsible for finding the hot topics and promoting the eBook, while your partner writes the eBook.

You can also partner with different people on different eBooks. You can target experts in different fields and partner with them to co-author books. Most experts don't like to write, but they are full of valuable content that they want to get out to the world. They can easily send you their best content and you can put it to paper in a way that the reader will love, and create a bestseller in the process.

If you choose this option, just make sure there is a joint venture contract describing how you will work together, what each of you will contribute and what the profit share agreement will look like.

Designing Your EBook

The last aspect of passively producing your book is the design of your book. Designing an eBook can be time consuming, especially in regards to designing the layout of your book and converting your manuscript to the Kindle format. But, just like writing your eBook, there are very talented people in the market place that you can hire to design your book as well.

My practice is to hire a contractor on Fiverr.com to design the layout of my book, and convert it into Kindle format for only $5. If there are additional artistic elements that I believe will create a greater experience for a reader, I will spend more. But, generally designing a great eBook has never cost me more than $20, even with the extra bells and whistles. And, if you really want to be hands-off, you can use the same professional or hire another to upload your eBook to Kindle for $5 as well.

CHAPTER 12

Becoming a Bestseller on Kindle

You've may have heard many authors talking about becoming a bestseller on Kindle. But why all the fuss? The most important reason to be a bestseller on Kindle, is that the better position you have on the bestseller list (spots numbered 1—6), the more exposure your eBook will get. And the more exposure you get, the more sales you get, and the greater the stream of income you create from selling eBooks on Kindle.

The second benefit of being a bestseller is that it will create a consistent or increasing amount of sales over time for you. You see, once you get on the bestseller list, then more people will buy your eBook. The more sales, the more your eBook will stay on the bestseller list, which again generates more sales, and so on. From my experience, being a bestseller is the single greatest influence on the success of your Kindle EBook business.

Last, being a bestseller also means instant prestige. Once people find out you are an author, but also an author that has sold books that are bestsellers, then any subsequent books you write will have an easier time selling and getting on the bestseller lists themselves. Not to mention all of the speaking gigs, coaching clients, media interviews that you will get as well.

So how does an author become a bestseller on Kindle? The answer is a lot simpler and easier than you think. Generally, to become a bestseller you need to:

1. **Find A Hot Topic People Are Hungry For.**

2. **Create A Kick Butt EBook People Will Love.**

3. **Get Tons of Five Star Reviews.**

4. **Price Your EBook for Maximum Sales.**

5. **Promote Your EBook to The Right Audience.**

Best Seller Tip #1—Creating a Kick Butt EBook People Will Love

Since we have already talked about how to find a hot eBook topic in previous chapters, I want to focus on how to create a kick butt eBook people will love.

In the non-fiction world, the most valued asset that people are looking for when they read an eBook is valuable, actionable content that really works. In other words, they want the advice that they know they can apply right away and get the results you promise.

This is the biggest reason that I rarely write about a topic, or give advice that I haven't proven myself. You see, readers highly value advice that has been proven to work. Why? Because they want to confidently know that that the advice you give them will work for them as well. And, this proof doesn't have to only come from your life your life either. It can come from the experience of others, or from tests that others have undergone to prove that it does work.

If you focus on giving readers content about effective, user-friendly best practices that bring great results, you will never fail getting raving fans for your eBook. Remember, they picked up your book because they are interested in your topic. And if you give them the best advice out there that works, not only will they love you for it, but they will tell the world about you as well.

Best Seller Tip #2—Get Tons of Reviews

The Holy Grail in Amazon Kindle is getting great, five star reviews for your eBook. This is because most Amazon customers make their buying choices based on the experience of other people. They don't want to risk buying an eBook, reading it and then finding out it was terrible. They want to save time and money by seeing how other people responded to it, and then make their choice whether they will buy it or not.

Why five star reviews? There are few reasons. The most important is that the Amazon Kindle customers rarely read the reviews, but rather, just check how many stars a book has. The second reason is that if you do get the dreaded negative review (and you will), all of the five star reviews you have will dilute the impact of the negative review. The last reason is that one of the criteria Amazon uses to determine who they will put on their bestseller list are the amount of positive reviews you have. If you have many, it will more guarantee a spot on the coveted bestseller list.

So how do you get great reviews for your eBook? The easiest way is to give our eBook away for free in exchange for a review. You can give a free copy of your eBook to friends, family, business associates, neighbors, etc. to read it and give you a review. Now you can't ask people to give you a five star review. But generally, since these first customers usually like you, there is a great chance that they will give you a glowing, five star review, anyway.

They don't even have to read the entire book to review it. They can just the read a couple of pages and tell about how much they are impressed, or interested in the book. They don't even have to own the eBook to review either. You can have it on your smartphone and let them read some of it, then ask them to go online and give you a review of the eBook so far. But a review from a purchased eBook, called a "verified review," carries a lot more weight in Amazon Kindle, so it's usually best to ask them to spend a few bucks to buy it, and then review.

Eventually, when you have enough reviews, your eBook builds enough momentum for the eBook to get its own reviews from customers that have purchased it. From my experience, the magic number to create enough momentum to jumpstart reviews for your book is between 10 and 20. So if you can get 10—20 friends, family, co-workers, etc. to review your book, it will create the kind of momentum it needs to get it on the bestseller list.

Bestseller Tip #3—Price Your eBook for Maximum Sales

In order to get the most sales for your eBook you need to price it in such a way that hundreds and thousands of customers will jump at the chance at buying your book. You have two options for this. You can either price for momentum or price for consistent sales.

Pricing for momentum is basically pricing your eBook at such a low price that it motivates more and more customers to buy. In the

Kindle marketplace, the ideal price for this, is to price your book at either $.99—$1.99. If you write a book on a hot topic, with valuable content, and lots of great five star reviews, and then price your book at $.99, it will fly off the shelves and easily put you on the bestseller list. Though I prefer $.99, it can still do just as well priced at $1.99. It's your choice, but personally I would test both to see which gives me the best result.

Eventually, you want to price your book for consistent sales. This is the price that will give you the best profit, and that will continue to motivate customers to buy. The ideal price for consistent sales in Kindle is $2.99. This is the standard price that customers usually spend for eBooks and the price that will bring you the most consistent profit. Now, you can price your eBook at $9.99, because you are convinced it is worth that, but you'll probably only get 1 to 2 sales a month. Or you can price at $2.99 and make 10—20 sales a day, and create a consistent stream of passive income for yourself.

The $2.99 price is also the price that will give you the most consistent profit in Kindle. It will generally net you about $2.00 in profit for each sale. Compared to publishing a paperback book through a place like Amazon CreateSpace, which only yields about $2—$3 in profit, I think that is pretty darn good. Especially because by using the system in this book you can produce a book with 1/5th of the time and effort it takes to create a full-length paperback book.

Bestseller Tip #4—Promote Your Kindle eBook

One of the benefits of using the system we've described so far, is that if you pick a hot topic that readers are hungry for, if you create valuable content that brings results; and if you get tons of five star reviews, as well as price for maximum sales, you will have to do very little promotion in order to get your eBook on the bestseller list. Personally, I've had two books on the bestseller list that didn't require me to promote them at all. But if you want to promote your eBook to the public, here is one of the best strategies for promoting your eBook successfully:

1. **Promote Through the Kindle Direct Publishing Select Program.** One of the most effective ways to promote your eBook is to join the Kindle Direct Publishing Select Program and launch your book with a five-day free promotion. With this program you can offer your book for free for five days every 90 days. You can promote your book for five days straight or promote it for a few days each week.

2. **Promote Your EBook on Free Book Promotion Sites.** The best places to promote your book during your free book promotion time, is to go online and find Free Book Promotion sites. These sites are designed to promote your Kindle eBook during your free promotion days to their database of thousands of readers. The result is that you get your book out to thousands of people in a short period of time. This also provides you with more reviews for your book from people that have read it for themselves.

The best result of this approach is that after your promotion, the momentum will allow you to price your eBook regularly and generate massive sales. The ideal price after a free promotion is $.99, which will keep the momentum going for your book sales. After you reach the bestseller list, especially the first 6 spots for your category, you can then go back to standard pricing, and continue to sell high volumes of eBooks.

Therefore, if you want to reach the bestseller list on kindle, the steps are not rocket science, but they are strategic and focused. And, if you put the time and effort, there is no reason why every eBook you produce cannot be a bestseller on Kindle. Most of all, the more exposure you get, then the more sales you get, will mean the greater the passive income stream you will get from all of your efforts selling eBooks on Kindle.

CHAPTER 13

Growing Your Kindle EBook Business to Grow Your Income

I'm sure you're wondering how to grow your Kindle EBook business, to not just make $500 a month, but rather make $5000 a month. Well, each Kindle eBook you sell will make you anywhere from $500 to $1,000 per eBook, per month. If you're really popular, you may even make $2,000 a month. Therefore, the simplest way to grow your Kindle eBook business is to simply make more books. If you repeat this process every one to three months, you can create 5—6 eBooks in a year and easily make $5000 a month. If you hire a great ghostwriter, and put out 10—20 titles a year, you can even clear $100K a year in passive income.

The best part is, once you write a book, you never have to work in order to make money with that eBook again. Though you may promote it a little bit here and there, or you may improve your eBook over time, the work is pretty much done after you hit the publish button. This makes this kind of work a great passive income stream that will eventually lead you to your financial freedom goal.

Right now, there are plenty of people that make their living off of creating Kindle eBooks. They have anywhere from 20 and 50 eBooks, and they are the bestsellers in their categories. The best part is that there are still thousands of opportunities for you to produce bestselling eBooks and create a great income for yourself too.

Does that sound like a good plan to you?

Kindle Recap and Resources

In conclusion, so how do you make money off successfully selling eBooks Kindle? Pick a hot subject for your e-book. Test and validate your eBook before you produce it. Passively produce your eBook through a ghostwriter or partner. Get great reviews for your eBook from friends, your family, and your associates. Promote your eBook for free through promotion sites on the Internet. Price it right for maximum sales. And then do it again and again until you make enough passive income to reach your financial freedom goal.

Here are a few resources I mentioned that will help you on your journey:

1. **Fiverr—**Fiverr.com. Just go there to find really great people to write your book, to design your covers, etc.

2. **Elance—**Elance.com. You will find great ghostwriters here at an affordable price.

3. **Transcription.** GMRTranscription.com. They will take your video or audio files and transcribe them. GMR Transcription is the best that I've seen so far that does this, with a 98% accuracy rate, so you won't have to edit that much.

4. **Keyword research.** Freshkey.com, and MerchantWords.com are both great if you want to find out what people are searching for on Amazon. For free general Internet search information use the Google Adwords Keyword Planner at https://adwords. google.com/KeywordPlanner.

If you would like a more detailed and step-by-step training on making money selling eBooks on Kindle, then consider my Udemy video course titled: **"Make $500—$5000 Passively Selling EBooks on Kindle,"** which you can find at this link.

https://www.udemy.com/make-passive-income-selling-kindle-ebooks.

Normally it retails for $149, but as a bonus for reading this book, you can get the course for $49 by using the coupon code: PENAPROMO49.

Now let's look at one of my favorite ways to make another $1K—$10K a month in passive income. This is the strategy that really jumpstarted my passive income efforts, and the one I think will do the same for you.

PART 3

Passive Income Idea #3: Amazon

This section is designed to give you a system that will provide you with an extra $1,000 to $10,000 a month in passive income by selling your own products on Amazon. The idea is that you are going to learn how to utilize the many automated systems, technology, and resources provided by Amazon in order to sell physical products and make money, yet using very little of your own resources.

I'm sure you've heard a lot of things about selling on Amazon. Yet, one thing we are not going to be talking about is retail arbitrage. Retail arbitrage is just the fancy way of saying to "buy low and then sell high." You've probably seen a lot of people scrambling at different discount thrift stores trying to buy things and then try to sell them on Amazon. This is not what we are going to talk about here. Instead I am going to show you how, by selling your own products, you can expect a return on investment of 100, even 200 percent, or more. This is because when you sell your own products with your own brand name, you'll be able to consistently create enough value that you can charge very high prices for your products.

Now if you are anything like me, you're probably thinking, "Am I going to have to hold a ton of inventory in my home?" The answer is no. You don't have to. Because Amazon provides you with great solutions for this, so that you will never have to store inventory in your own home ever again.

So if this sounds good to you, strap yourself in and get ready for an exciting ride through the jungles of the Amazon…

CHAPTER 14

How to Successfully Sell Your Own Products on Amazon— An Overview

Now, what does it take in order to be successful at selling products on Amazon? Here is an overview of the Amazon Sales Success System I am going to share with you in this section:

1. **Identify Desirable Products**—You will learn how to find great products that people will be eager to buy.

2. **Create A Unique Brand**—You will learn how to take any generic product, add a very powerful brand to it, and create a substantial amount of value that people want to pay for.

3. **Find High Quality Product Sources**—You are going to learn how to find great places where you can source high quality products to sell on Amazon.

4. **Create a High Converting Amazon Listing**—You will learn how to write the most emotionally compelling listing that will compel people to buy.

5. **Test And Validate Your Product**—You are going to learn how to test your product in the Amazon marketplace, to make sure that you find the product that you will be able to sell a lot of, and make big profit from.

6. **Automate Your Amazon Business**—You will learn how to use the tools Amazon provides you, to cut down the amount of time, effort, resources, and money you spend, but still continue to make a large profit.

CHAPTER 15

Identifying Products That Sell

Now let's talk about the first part of the Amazon selling process, identifying a desirable product. How do you find the best type of products that people will want to buy? Well, it simply takes two things:

1. **Establishing the right product criteria.**
2. **Finding the hottest selling products on the Amazon Bestseller List.**

Establishing the Best Product Criteria

You need to be able to pick the best product criteria that will guarantee the most success of your Amazon selling business. This is the "strategic planning" part of your Amazon business.

Now, you could jump on Amazon right now, see what the bestsellers are, pick some products, source and sell them, and then fall flat on your face. Why? Because even though you did all the work, you didn't foresee the challenges that could come up because you picked the wrong product, picked the wrong product category, or the timing was wrong.

So, what I want to do is give you a general overview of some good product criteria that can help you have the best chance at finding and successfully selling products on Amazon:

1. **Weight**—You're going to be having these products shipped to you from other places, and you're also going to ship them to customers as well. When you ship these products you want to make sure that you won't lose all your profit on shipping fees. Therefore, in order to reduce shipping costs substantially, it's generally best to have most of the products that you sell be less than 5 pounds.

2. **Liability**—It's best to minimize liability as much as possible. So stay away from anything that has any type of risk potential. I don't sell wood stoves, for obvious reasons. Those could turn around and actually hurt the customer and the customer could come back and sue me. I also try to avoid baby products. In other words, anything that could potentially cause people harm, I generally stay away from.

3. **Price**—I generally try to find products that I can sell between $20 and $200. Personally, I tend to go after higher priced products because I try to create enough of a valuable brand that people can justify spending a lot for it. But a $20 product can be just as good, especially if it only cost you only a couple

of dollars to produce. And if a large group of people buys them, you can create a very lucrative business for yourself.

4. **Size**—I also try to find products that are small in size. Why? Because they're easy to pack, and easy to ship. Try to avoid odd shaped products, even if they are light. If you find a light-weight product but it's long, like a tennis racket, then you're going to find it difficult to find packaging for it.

5. **Minimal Moving Parts**—I also try to find products with minimal moving parts. Why? Because the more moving parts you have, the greater the chance the product has for breaking down. Then, the more chances you have of your customer coming back to you and asking for a refund. So, try to avoid those too.

6. **Generic**—For your Amazon selling business, you are going to focus on products that are very generic in nature. This is because the more generic they are, the easier you can add your own brand, your logo, and make slight changes to the product so that it becomes a unique product that is your own. Then, after that, you can pretty much charge whatever you want as long as you can show people the value that the product has in their lives. Generic products are the products I will be focusing on mostly in this book.

7. **Easy to Source**—This means high quality items that you can find many suppliers for. If you find a great product, but no suppliers, then you've wasted your time. Or if you find a great product but very few suppliers for it, then you are at the mercy of whatever your supplier charges you. You want to find products that you can find multiple suppliers for so that you can negotiate the best

rates for your product. Later on in this book, I'm going to show you exactly how to do this.

The Amazon Bestseller List—Shooting Fish in a Barrel

There is no better place to identify hot products than on the Amazon Best Seller List.

The best strategy to find hot products to sell, is to go through each major category on the Amazon Bestseller List looking for the products that meet the product criteria that you create.

I generally start looking for products in the Amazon Bestseller main categories, then I will go into subcategories. The best part of going into subcategories, is that you can find some really interesting, but profitable niches, with little competition, which you can later dominate.

Here are the steps that I take when I search for potential hot products on Amazon:

1. **Go to the Amazon Bestseller List.** You can find it on this link: www.amazon.com/Best-Sellers/zgbs. Or do a search on Google for "Amazon Bestseller List" and you will easily find it.

2. **Choose a Product Category.** On the left of the screen, you will find a list of main product categories. Choose a product category where you will find the most generic products that fit your criteria. This will usually include most categories, but generally I focus on the following:

    • Automotive (for their accessories).

    • Camera and Photo.

- Home and Kitchen.

- Home Improvement.

- Kitchen and Dining.

- Musical Instruments.

- Patio, Lawn and Garden.

- Pet supplies.

- Sports and Outdoors.

3. **Keep A List.** Open an excel file, and as you look for products through the main category that fit your product criteria, copy and paste product titles and prices into your excel file.

4. **Search Subcategories too.** After you finish going through the main category, go through the subcategories and do the same (there are 100 products per category).

5. **Rinse, and Repeat.** Then move on the next main category on the list (I'll usually go 3—4 categories deep), and go through the process again.

6. **Choose Some Test Products.** When you are done going through the different main categories and subcategories, go through your list on excel, and choose 10—20 products you determine are the best out of the list. Start sourcing those first.

This process should result in helping you find 10—20 really great products that you can now begin to find suppliers for. You now also have a whole list of products you can go back to, once you get your first products successfully selling, to look for new products to sell in the future.

CHAPTER 16

Creating a Unique Brand

In this chapter we are going to talk about how to create a unique brand. The best way to describe what a brand is, is that a brand is the name and logo that inspires a specific feeling in your customers, that ultimately motivates them to buy. In other words, a brand creates so much value in the mind of your customers, that they will feel highly motivated to spend all types of money to buy your product.

To be clear, this entire system hinges on your ability to create a unique and valuable brand for your product. This is because you can have an incredibly outstanding product, but if customers aren't able to see the value, they won't purchase it. On the other hand, if you create a unique enough brand, and a unique enough experience in the customer's mind, they will be emotionally compelled to buy that product, and tell their friends about it. That is why in this book I focus more on selling your own products. You see, you can take a very generic product, add a powerful brand to it, and then all of a sudden you have people spending all kinds of money on your product.

So, let's look at a few different criteria that it takes to create a unique and valuable brand:

1. **Establishing a Unique Selling Proposition (USP)**—This is the one feature of your product that makes it unique, different, and better than everyone else's, so that customers will be willing to spend money on your product.

2. **Choosing the Ideal Name for Your Brand**—If you pick the right name for your brand, it can motivate people to feel good and to emotionally compel them to purchase your product.

3. **Designing the Ideal Logo.** The purpose of a logo is to choose the right image that puts the right perspective in the customer's mind that will emotionally compel them to buy.

4. **Picking the Ideal Name for Your Product**—It creates a powerful experience for customers when a product has a name. It's not enough that the car is a Honda or a Toyota, but people appreciate it more if it's a Honda Pilot or Toyota Camry.

5. **Designing the Ideal Packaging.** Designing the ideal packaging is the difference between getting something in the mail wrapped in bubble wrap and then getting something in the mail with a very glossy, good looking box that makes you feel like, "Wow! I just bought something of value."

6. **Creating the Ideal Experience**—This includes creating the best experience for customers that puts them in the perfect emotional state, that'll make it very easy for them to take out their credit cards and buy.

Establishing a Unique Selling Proposition (USP)

So how do you create a unique selling proposition for your product? Well, for every product, I first start by trying to find the answer to this question: "What will make my product different, unique, and better than everyone else's?"

Since we're working with a generic product, we want to make it stand out from everyone else's. Now, it doesn't have to be something that makes it better than everyone else's, it just needs to be unique. Because uniqueness creates value in the mind of your customer.

In order to find a USP for my product, the first thing I like to do is to pick a particular feature of the product to work with. I start with a list of all of the different features and attributes of the product, and then I choose one specific feature that my competitors are not focusing on, that will be valuable to my customer. Then I turn that one unique feature into my unique selling proposition.

Finding a Great USP

So where do you go to find a great USP? One of the best places to start is to look at your competitors. You start by finding a competitor that is selling a similar product you are considering. Then you look at all of their reviews, focusing especially on the reviews that are three stars and below. Look at what their customers are saying, specifically focusing on what their customers are complaining about. Now they could be complaining about a missing component. Or maybe they wish the product came with a particular accessory.

When you hear a lot of people complaining about the same things, make a list of these complaints, and choose one of them to make your unique selling proposition. You already know your customers are looking for it, and you also know that your competition is lacking it; so, you can go ahead and pick that feature and make it your USP. Next thing you know, you will quickly stand out from your competition, and collect the lion's share of business.

Creating the Ideal Brand Name

You can turn a generic product into a unique brand that people will remember, by simply giving it the best brand name. The brand name not only conveys the product's unique features and benefits, but it sends the message to the customer that it is a valuable product that can meet their needs.

But how does one go about picking a great name for your brand? Well it starts by first asking yourself the question, "What feeling or emotion do I want to convey to my customer when they think about my product?" Whatever that feeling is, it should give you an idea of what direction you want to go when you pick the name for your brand. For example, if you are selling fun pet toys, you want your brand name to be something that makes people think about pet's having fun. Something like, "Witty Kitty Pet Toys," or "Merry Jerry Pet Toys," even, "AniMotion Pet Toys," could work.

So your brand name should create the feeling for your customers that says you can meet their needs or fulfill their desires. And by doing so, you will attract hundreds of customers to buy more from you than your competitors.

Choosing a Kick Butt Brand Name

The quickest way to find a great brand name, is to look at the competitors that are already selling similar products. As you look at their brand name, you must understand that they have already put the time, the effort, even the money to come up with that great brand. Why not find a name that conveys the same message as theirs, but uses different words? This is where a Thesaurus comes in really handy.

Here are the steps you can use to choose a great brand name:

1. **First take your competitor's brand name, and look up at that name in a Thesaurus.**

2. **Review the other words to see if there are other ways of conveying the exact same message, with a really cool sounding word, that will appeal to customers.**

3. **Test it out with others and see if they get the message you are trying to convey.**

You'll be amazed at how many really great words pop up, which you can use for your brand name.

Designing the Ideal Logo

A great brand also requires a great logo. And just like a great brand conveys a valuable message to the customer, so a great logo confirms that message.

So, you want to choose colors, fonts, and a design, that will lead the customer to emotionally connect with your brand and unique selling proposition. For example, if your brand name is Frolic Pet

Toys, you want to pick colors that are compatible with that band. Light colors like: white, light blue, yellow, green (nature), etc., will work great. On the other hand, in this instance, you would stay away from dark colors like black, grey, or dark brown, because they have the opposite effect on the customer.

The idea behind this, is that just like people are influenced by words and pictures, people are influenced by colors and visual designs also.

Now, if you're like me, you may be thinking, "I don't have an artistic bone in my body!" or "I don't know what colors to choose!" This is where you can go to a place like Fiverr.com or Elance.com and find an affordable graphic designer to design your logo for you. You can give them your brand name, your USP and any other information that will help them design a great logo. You can even send them a couple of examples of competitor logos that you really like and see what they come up with. For best results, pay $5 each to three graphic designers on Fiverr.com and have them all design a logo for you. When you receive all three, pick the best one.

Coming Up With a Valuable Product Name

How about the product name itself? How do you pick a unique product name that will add even more value to your product? Well, again, the value is found in uniqueness. Just like your USP, the more unique the product name you choose, the more valuable it will be, and the higher the price you can charge.

There is a reason that car companies give cars names. A Toyota Camry, or a Honda Pilot is a lot more valuable than a car named, "The beige Toyota that is parked over there." And just like cars, once you give a product its own unique name, the sticker price can increase by thousands of dollars.

So how do you come up with great product names? I always say start by focusing on a specific product name that will highlight that product's USP. Another place to start is to look at what your competitors are doing. See what they're calling their products then use a thesaurus to get multiple variations of that name. Then test it with your product and see how people respond.

Choosing the Ideal Product Packaging

Just like your brand and your logo, your packaging should also highlight your unique selling proposition. For example if your brand and pet toy product name is "The Frolic Tuffball," you're not going to put it in a black box with silver words on it. It just won't give it the right feeling. Rather, a nice green and white box with a picture of a boy throwing a "Frolic Tuffball," as a golden retriever chases after it, in the park, on a sunny day, will probably highlight the USP best.

Again, the easiest place to look for great packaging ideas is your competitors. See what they're doing and try to do something similar, but make it unique to what your unique selling proposition is. As for the actual box or container you will use, look at what your competitors use. You can copy the type of box or container they use, just change the labeling on it with your brand name, product name logo and colors.

This is where Fiverr.com and Elance.com come to the rescue, again. You can hire a package designer for as low as five bucks. For example, I hired someone at Fiverr.com to design the packaging for one of my products, and I was completely blown away by what they designed. For only five bucks, I got the most incredible package box that I am using to this day. I even gave the guy an extra few dollars because he did such a great design.

Creating the Ideal Customer Experience

Let's now talk about creating the ideal experience for the customer. If you provide anything extra with your product, it generally enhances your customer's experience and therefore the value of your product. The type of extras I mean are any type of accessories or bonuses that your customer can get with your product.

Customers love accessories, and they love free accessories even more. By identifying compatible accessories, sourcing them cheaply and adding them to your product, it will allow you to not only increase the value of the product, but give you the option to increase the price.

Bonuses also create a better experience for your customers. By adding a free EBook download with the purchase of your product, it may be what pushes your risk averse customer into finally making the decision to buy. You can deliver that bonus in the form of a little card that you put in with your product packaging. The card will direct them to your website, where they download their free EBook and join your email list.

These all will help you not only create a great experience for your customers, but also, by adding those things that your competitors are missing, it will help you stand out and become a bestseller very quickly.

CHAPTER 17

Finding High Quality Product Sources

Let's now talk about finding high quality product sources. I mention high quality because there are a lot of wholesalers out there who will sell you all kinds of junk. But we want to focus on the highest quality products. Why? Because we want to help our customers be satisfied. And there's nothing that satisfies customers more than having high quality products that meet their needs that last, and that they can brag to their friends about.

Also, you want to be proud of the things that you're selling. You want to look forward to selling your product to customers and feel like you can stand behind your product. So again, it is critical to only sell the highest quality products, and that means finding high quality product sources.

But where do you go to find wholesale sources for high quality products? Well, in this chapter we are going to learn:

1. **How to find high quality product suppliers in China and communicate effectively with them.**

2. **How to sample and test your products.**

3. **Negotiating prices and terms with suppliers.**

Finding High Quality Product Sources

So, where do you go to find high quality wholesale product sources? Well, the good news is that in our modern world the Internet has made it very easy for us. There are two very powerful search engines created for finding wholesale sources in China that I am going to talk about, and which we will focus on in this book. One of them is AliExpress, which is the Amazon of China. The other one is Alibaba, which is the behemoth of all wholesale service providers in China and the world.

Now, of course, there are many more product suppliers in the US and many other countries. But I want to focus on these two, specifically, because they're the most user-friendly, they're the ones most used by Americans to source products overseas, and these are the ones that I have successfully used. I want to share with you what works for me so that you can start immediately making multiple streams of income sourcing and selling products on Amazon.

Alibaba

Alibaba.com is China's and the world's biggest online commerce company. Its main sites Taobao, Tmall, Aliexpress and Alibaba.com have hundreds of millions of users, and host millions of merchants and businesses. Alibaba handles more business than any other e-commerce company. Alibaba is also the most popular destination for online shopping, in the world's fastest growing e-commerce market.

It hosts the greatest list of wholesale suppliers where you can source an abundance of products to sell on Amazon. Alibaba's user-friendly website, makes it easy to find suppliers because it allows you to filter out suppliers according to your criteria. Alibaba also filters out suppliers based on their own quality standards, which more guarantees that you will find a quality supplier for your product.

AliExpress

AliExpress.com is the retail division of Alibaba, and is focused on small volume orders of "ready-made" products designed for the medium and small importers who can't afford to buy a large container of goods.

Since most of the same suppliers from Alibaba are the sellers of retail items on Aliexpress, you can still obtain wholesale pricing for "made to order" products, by contacting sellers on Aliexpress directly and asking them for wholesale pricing.

But why go to AliExpress when you are dealing with the same wholesalers as Alibaba? The reason I go to AliExpress is that you get good feedback information from customers that have previously purchased retail items from these suppliers. This gives you even more data as to the quality of the supplier's products.

Sourcing Products Effectively

The process for sourcing products on Alibaba and AliExpress, is a very straightforward one. It starts by asking the right sourcing questions. Here are the questions I generally email suppliers when I am inquiring about their product:

1. **What is the price per piece for bulk orders?**—I ask this question because sometimes they don't exactly tell you the price for bulk orders, or the price that is listed on the website is outdated.

2. **Do you have the product available?** Sometimes they may not have the product readily available in stock. They may have to manufacture it. It might even take up to 14 to 45 days to produce. You need to know this so you can understand your timeframe.

3. **How long will it take to have it ready to ship?**—Again, you want to know exactly how much time it will take the product to reach you so you can get your products to your customers.

4. **What is the minimum order quantity (MOQ)?** For many suppliers, they don't want to do business with you unless they know you're going to buy a certain amount. You want to make sure that you have enough capital to buy the minimum amount quantity set by suppliers. The good news is that suppliers are generally flexible about the minimum order quantity if they know you will buy from them consistently over a long time.

5. **What is the shipping cost for the minimum order quantity?** When they ship you the minimum order quantity, you want to make

sure you know exactly how much it costs to ship from overseas. Also, you need this so you can calculate what your exact expense will be, which allows to project the exact return on investment you will have for every sale you make.

6. **What are your price tiers and quantity discounts?** Sometimes if you buy more they'll give you more discounts. Get this information up front so you can later plan your inventory in such a way that you can get more discounts.

7. **Can you send me the label or package design template?** Why do I want this? Because I can take the supplier's design template and add my logo to it. Then I can have the supplier print my packaging for me at no extra cost. So you can take the design template, ask a graphic designer on Fiverr.com to add your logo to it and send it back to your supplier to print.

8. **Can you add my logo to your unit (a.k.a.: OEM)?** I want my logo to not just to be on the packaging, I like it to actually be on the actual product itself. This way people can know that it's our product. Granted, you can get away with a product without a logo and just have your logo on the packaging. But if you want to build a brand, it has more value when people can actually see your logo every time they pick up the product.

9. **What is the price and shipping cost for a sample?** We need to sample the product before we buy from the supplier. We also need samples to test and validate the product on Amazon. You want to know the cost for samples and shipping so you can add this to your budget. Expect the shipping cost to be high for one sample, so you may want to order five to ten samples at a time.

This allows you to thoroughly sample the product and to have product that you can test right away on Amazon.

Sampling and Testing

Sampling and testing is by far one of the most important parts of wholesale sourcing. Though it is tempting to avoid this step, I tell you from personal experience, that if you try to sell a product that you have not thoroughly sampled and tested, you are in for a world of trouble.

So when you test your samples, test as if you were a consumer. Use your critical eye. Look at it like you just spent $10, $50 or $200 on this product. Look at it in this way because that is what your customers are going to be doing. Make sure you test for quality, durability, user-friendliness, and aesthetics. Ask others to test the samples and give you honest feedback too.

And if you feel any reservations during the testing period, it is a red flag to not sell that product. As a matter of fact, do not sell that product until you feel completely confident that the product is of the highest of quality.

Negotiating Rates and Terms

Once you approve the samples it's time to negotiate the best rates and the quantities you need from your supplier. Although suppliers put their prices and minimum order quantities on the Alibaba or AliExpress website, they are not fixed in stone. Suppliers are generally very flexible because they want to establish a long-term business relationship with you.

Your goal is to get the best price possible, without reducing the quality of your product. Personally, I don't mind paying the highest price for a high quality product because I know I can sell it for three, four, or even five times as much and make a great profit from it. Even though I spend a little bit more, it doesn't matter, because my customer is happy, the supplier is happy and I'm happy. So don't be cheap.

CHAPTER 18

Creating a High Converting Listing

Creating a high converting Amazon listing is one of the most crucial steps in successfully selling on Amazon. Why? Because this is your advertising page. This is the page that people are going to come to and determine whether they see enough value in your product to pull out their wallet and buy from you.

So how does one create a high converting listing? High converting listings are created using a few key components, including:

1. **Creating the best converting title for your product.**

2. **Adding emotionally compelling images that will motivate people to buy.**

3. **Writing high converting bullets and descriptions that motivate people to purchase your product.**

4. **Providing valuable bonuses to motivate customers to make the decision to buy from you.**

Creating a High Converting Title

The title is the main description of your product. There are few criteria that make a really high converting product title. And the great thing about Amazon is that it gives you a lot of room to add a whole lot of other words to really beef up you title. Here are a few elements that make for a high converting title:

1. **Your Brand**—You want the brand name in your title, because eventually your brand is going to become popular enough that people actually look for you.

2. **Your Product Name**—Put your product's unique name in the title, next to your brand, so that you can create immediate value in the mind of your customer. For example, if you are selling baking products, you would put your brand, "Baker's Delight," next to your product's unique name, "Fascinating Cupcake Liners," at the start of your title.

3. **Product Description**—People want to make sure they know what they're buying, so make sure you let them know, that they are in the right place by giving a clear description of what you are selling.

4. **Your USP**—You want to add your USP in the title because it is the one thing that makes you stand out from your competition, and the unique selling proposition that tells your customers that your product is better or different from everyone else's.

   Personally, I like to put the USP in all caps so that people will not miss it.

5. **Product Benefits**—You want to add the greatest benefits your product brings so that customer will be immediately motivated to either buy your product, or read more of your listing. Going with our previous example, your title will end up looking like this (this is an actual product that is currently the Amazon Bestseller in its category and an example of a great title; I've just changed the brand name):

> "Baker's Delight Fascinating Silicone Baking Cups—Set of 12 Reusable Cupcake Liners in Six Vibrant Colors in Storage Container—Muffin, Gelatin, Snacks, Frozen Treats, Ice Cream or Chocolate Shell-lined Dessert Molds—Great for Bento Lunch Boxes—BPA Free Food Grade Silicone Non-stick Bake ware—VIBRANT SILICONE BAKING CUPS."

Look at all of the benefits it conveys—Reusable, Vibrant colors, Great for Bento Lunch Boxes, Non-stick—BPA Free, etc.

Now some people will tell you not to add so much in the title. But after continual testing, it is pretty obvious that the more benefits you add to the title, the more people will buy. This is because the benefits motivate the person to continue to read my description and think, "Wow! This product has everything I've been looking for." That's the response I want people to have, so I'll add as many benefits as Amazon will allow in the title.

6. **Keywords**—I also list keywords in the title. Why? Because search engines do find those Amazon pages as well. So I will use a keyword tool to identify the most popular keywords for my product both in the search engines and in Amazon. Google Keyword Planner, FreshKey, or MerchantWords are

good services you can use to find the most popular product words.

When using keywords, you also have to make sure that it fits well with your product title, so that it can both motivate customers to buy, but also be easily found by search engines. In other words, string it together in such a way that people feel like it just flows well.

Use Emotionally Compelling Images

Another critical area to success of your Amazon listing, is the use of emotionally compelling Amazon images. Every Amazon listing is required to have a picture; and if you don't have one, it keeps your product from being listed in their general product category listing.

But if you want to create a high converting listing, it's not enough just to have a picture. You have to make sure you have an emotionally compelling picture that motivates people to buy. Also, one picture is not enough. If you want people to buy, you need to fill it up with six to eight high quality pictures.

How do you choose an emotionally compelling image to use? You want to make sure you get images that show a lot of the benefits that people are going to get from buying the product. You want the kind of images that give them a glimpse of how happy they will be from using the product. In other words, what the product is going to do for them, the product in action, and the product in the best light possible.

Product Bullets and Descriptions

The Product Description is a combination between the bulleted description and the main product description. The bulleted description is the bulleted list of information that is under the product title and to the right of the image. The main description is the main area toward the middle of the page under the title "Product Description."

In order to create high converting bullet points, I generally focus on just making sure you add as many benefits as you can. I also put the title of the bullet in all caps and the details in regular letters. This way it can really stand out for people who don't like to read the details. You also want to list the bullets in order of priority: the most valuable benefit first, then the next most valuable benefit, and so on. Also, for each bullet put as much information as possible and use up all of the character space Amazon gives you. The more detail the better, especially for customers that need to read the details to make a buying decision.

For the main product description in the middle of the page, I like to focus on the five P's. Now, the five P's are designed to focus on the five things that will help motivate the customer most to buy your product. The five P's include:

1. **The Problem**—Talk about their problem. Talk about the problem that your product fixes. Why? Because that is why they're coming to look at your product, they have an issue or conflict or something that they need fixing and they think your product can do it for them.

2. **The Promise**—Tell them what your product can do. List all of the benefits that your product promises and how it can alleviate

all their pain, help them be happier, help them be healthier, sexier, leaner, thinner, richer, whatever it is.

3. **The Picture**—Besides your product pictures, this is your opportunity to create mental pictures for them. Start describing what a vision of a better future using your product will look like. Describe it in visual words. Give them a story, give them an idea in their heads. Your actual pictures will help, but by describing it further to them it motivates them even more.

4. **The Proof**—Add supporting evidence that your product can fulfill on its promise, whether in the form of case studies, credentials, statistics, studies, and certifications. These will help the customer make a better decision because they feel like they are reducing their risk.

   Note: As of the writing of this book, Amazon does not allow testimonials in the product description; so stick to credentials, studies and certifications if you have them.

5. **The Push**—Make sure you encourage your customers to buy, by putting on the bottom of the description the direct suggestion to, "Buy Now!" or "Get yours today!"

   Many Amazon listings do not have this kind of call to action, and I don't understand why. But you need to put it in there and make it very commanding, so people can take action on all your suggestions.

Adding Valuable Bonuses

You may think that the title, images and description is enough to get a customer to buy. 80% of the time you would be right. But, people need as much reason to buy as possible, because price is usually an issue. So, if you can create enough value to outweigh the risk in buying, you will always have a sale.

So, add a lot of valuable bonuses. Give away many free bonuses that will make your product more valuable in the eyes of your customer. This includes valuable accessories. If you can add an accessory, throw it in there. It could be a case, it could be a wrist strap, it could be extra batteries, etc. If it is valuable in the eyes of your customer, add it in and your product will become even more valuable.

I like offering a free EBook download in my listing. They can get access to it through a postcard that I add in the product packaging. The postcard then sends the customer to a website to download their free eBooks. The benefit of this is that I can capture their contact information and add them on my email list for future promotions.

CHAPTER
19

Testing and Validation

The main purpose of testing and validation is to see if people even want your product. You can come up with the best product in the world, and find a great source for it; but if nobody wants your product, it's going to be a waste of your time and money.

This happens a lot to new Amazon Sellers. They believe that because they love their own product, then everyone else is going to want their product also. Ultimately, when they finally list their product, the reality hits when they realize they are not getting any sales.

On the contrary, the only way to truly know if your product will be successful is to test it in the marketplace. Only if you throw your product in the marketplace and people buy it with cold, hard cash, will you know if it will be successful.

Testing and validation is also essential to verify how effective your Amazon listing is. The more you tweak and test your listing, and the more buyer response you get, the closer you will be to finding the ideal listing that compels most customers to buy.

Pricing also benefits greatly from testing. The more you test different pricing levels, the closer you get to the ideal target price which will bring you the most customers and the most profit.

How to Test and Validate Your Products

This is the process that I follow to test products in the marketplace that has been very effective for me:

1. **Initially, order five samples from your supplier to test for quality.** This includes testing the samples to make sure that the product is high quality, durable, user-friendly, and that it is aesthetically pleasing (that it looks good). The reason I choose five samples is that sometimes the samples they send you are not the same as the products you will order in the future. By ordering five, I get a good idea of the product I will be working with. Also, I can verify if the quality is consistent with all of the samples.

2. **After you test your samples, order another 10—20 units to test on Amazon.** Once you confirm that the product is of high quality, then you need to test it in the marketplace. The idea is that if you can sell 10 units in a month, then there is a good chance that more people will want to buy your product. If you can't sell 10 units in a month, even after extensive testing, then that is confirmation that people will probably not want to buy your product.

3. **List the product on Amazon.** Use all of the different criteria we listed in previous chapters (title, images, description, and bonuses) and list the product. Since you are only testing, you don't have to go through all the process of expertly "Photoshopping"

images like I mentioned previously. At this point, the supplier's pictures will work just fine.

Test your titles by adding different benefits. Keep swapping out benefits in your title to see which one most resonates with people. Test the product name, too. Test your images by rotating images, or swapping out images to see which works best. Test your descriptions and bullet points by changing the five P's (The problem, the promise, the picture, the proof, the push). Test your bonuses. Try one downloadable book, or give them another one. Try one accessory, and if that doesn't work, try another accessory. Keep tweaking and testing, little by little, every day, until you find the listing that really resonates with customers (meaning that it will drive customers to buy).

4. **Test Your Pricing**—Choose whether you are going to price for momentum or price for value. Pricing for momentum includes pricing your product at a comparable or lower price to your competitors. Incrementally raise prices until the sales slowdown. Then go back to the previous level you were at that produced daily sales.

   Pricing for value means pricing it at a high price, and then lower your price incrementally until customers begin to buy daily.

5. **Packaging and Shipping**—Choose your preliminary packaging to fulfill and test orders. Now, it won't be the fancy packaging with your logo on it, but choose something that's nice. Then test the process of getting the orders, packaging the orders, sending out the orders to your customers and making sure your customers are happy. Prepare the inserts you will put in your

packaging; whether product materials, free bonuses, product instructions, etc.

When you test your packaging and shipping in this way, it shows you how good, or how fast you are in your ability to fulfill on orders.

6. **Feedback and Reviews**—Ask your first couple customers about how they feel about your products. "Did they like your product?" "What didn't they like about your product?" In other words, be very specific in the questions you ask your customers, and they'll be glad to tell you because they want a great product.

If they really liked your product, ask them for reviews. Begin to collect reviews that will help to build your product value and sales rank in Amazon.

Expectations When You're Testing

You can expect it to be about two to three weeks before you actually get your first sale. Sometimes, you can get sales right away (especially if you price for momentum), but don't be discouraged if you don't see a sale for two to three weeks.

Once you do get sales, remember the focus is testing, not on making money. You are only gathering data, so every situation is a learning opportunity. Everything that does not go the way you want it, is an opportunity for you to learn and more streamline your process.

Expect to wait 60 days to have enough data to determine if your product is a winner or a loser. Keep tweaking and testing everything until you start making daily sales, or until you conclude that there is no viable market for the product.

Validating All of Your Data

After you have gathered all of this information, how can you tell if your product passed the test? Here are the criteria I use to determine if I have a winning product on Amazon:

1. **Sales Validation**—If you can sell 10 products in a month, then you have a product that you can build a business around. If you can't get 10 sales in a month, then forget it. You probably don't have a product that people are interested in. Now this is good news, because it means you can avoid wasting time, but instead you can go out and look for another product and try it again.

2. **Price Validation**—How do I know if people will continue to buy at a certain price? If I can get two or three sales at a certain price point, within a span of a few days, then I feel confident that I can keep it at that price point and more will buy. One sale at a certain price may be a fluke. Two sales I feel better about. Three, four, five sales means that I've got something that's hot, and that I've found the right price point that will work for customers.

3. **Customer Satisfaction Validation**—How do you know if customers are satisfied? If you receive multiple four to five star reviews from verified purchasers, then you know your product is satisfying customers (a verified purchaser is someone who has actually bought your product and gives a review). Since only 10 percent of customers on Amazon give reviews, then you know you're doing something right and the customers are happy with the product.

CHAPTER 20

Automating Your Amazon Selling Business

We've talked about many things in this book, but wouldn't it be nice to be able to automate your entire Amazon Selling Business, so that you only have to work at it five to ten hours a month?

Well, there are many different resources you can use both through Amazon and outside of Amazon to greatly simplify and automate your Amazon Selling business. The idea is, that in each of these areas, you can automate each process so you save a lot of the extra time, effort, resources, and money you would normally use, but still continue to create a lot of revenue, income and profit.

Automating the Product Selection Process

One way you to automate the product selection process is by taking the product selection process I mentioned in the early parts of this book, and use it to train a virtual assistant to find ideal potential products for you, using your criteria. You can show them the step-by-step process, or you can make a video of the process, and then have them focus on finding products week per week in every category you are interested in. This way all you have to do is to review the products they find to see which is the best one for you to pursue.

You can find great virtual assistants on Elance.com or Odesk. com. You can even find a good assistant for $5 on Fiverr.com. Or you can get an intern from the local college to do it for you.

Automating the Sourcing Process

Just like the product selection process, you can train your virtual assistant on how to source products using the process I mentioned in the product-sourcing chapter of this book. They can go through Alibaba and AliExpress looking for great suppliers, and they can email the suppliers the sourcing questions. They can follow up on any correspondence with suppliers, and even request for samples from qualified suppliers. If you trust your assistant, you can even give them access to a petty cash account through a debit or credit card with a limit, and have them order samples for you. You will do the sample testing yourself, but if you train your assistant well, they may be able to do this as well.

Automating the Branding Process

For branding, you have the option to hire a branding specialist to help you come up with a great brand. It may be a small investment on your part, but the profitable result will justify the expense. Also you can go to Fiverr.com to find a graphic designer to help design your logo, packaging, etc.

Automating the Creation of High Converting Amazon Listings

You can find great people who specialize in Amazon listings. You can even find great copywriters that will apply their skills to your Amazon listing and get you great results. Personally, I have found some great Amazon Listing copywriters on Fiverr.com, and for $20 I was able to get a compelling title, bullets and description written for me for each product I have.

Automating the Fulfilment and Inventory Management Process

To automate the fulfillment and management process there is no greater solution than Fulfillment by Amazon (FBA). FBA is just the easiest, most cost effective way to do it, because Amazon has the entire fulfillment process down to a science.

FBA will store, pick, pack, and ship your inventory. They will notify you via email if your inventory is running low. They handle all customer service questions and any returns. They also provide all types of reports, to let you project your inventory needs. Not to mention they provide you with all types of support and tools to help you succeed. It truly is a no brainer.

In addition to using FBA, you can automate your fulfillment and inventory management even further by either training your supplier to ship directly to Amazon FBA for you; by hiring a third party fulfillment center to receive your products, prepare them and send them to FBA; or by hiring an independent contractor to do it for you.

Automating the Customer Satisfaction Process

For customer inquiries, you can have your virtual assistant respond to all customer inquiries and issues. Just train them to know exactly what to do, and to have the right attitude dealing with the customer so they're actually friendly, kind, and serviceable. Once this is done, the entire customer service process is automated and you don't have to do much of anything. Then all you have to do is collect a check. And if you use FBA, Amazon does all this for you.

Automating the Review Gathering Process

You can outsource the sending out of emails to customers asking for reviews, to a virtual assistant also. They can do it on a weekly basis, sending your customer review template to new customers within 14 days of their purchase. This gives you a great edge in the Amazon marketplace because other sellers on Amazon rarely do this.

Amazon Recap and Resources

So what does it take to successfully sell your own products on Amazon? It takes finding hot products people want. It takes creating a unique brand that people find value in and want to pay for. It takes finding wholesales sources that sell high quality products. It takes testing and validating your product so that you will know people really want what you have to offer. And, last, it takes automating your business by using all of the great resources Amazon provides.

So, with this Amazon Selling process you can begin to make anywhere from $1,000 to $10,000 a month on Amazon. No to mention, that you can fully automate the process so that you're working less than ten hours a month. From personal experience, the biggest reward you will find is that If you follow this system, you can even begin to see a profit in as little as 90 days. And ultimately, you will create a great passive income stream for yourself and your family that will continue to grow over time.

Here are a few additional resources for you that I mentioned in this section:

1. **Graphics and Amazon Listing**—Fiverr.com, Elance.com, Odesk.com.

2. **Sourcing**—Alibaba.com, AliExpress.com.

3. **Keyword Research**—Freshkey.com, MerchantWords.com, Adwords.com (Google Keyword Planner).

If you would like a more detailed and step-by-step training on making money selling your own products on Amazon, then consider my Udemy video course titled: **"Make $1K—$10K Selling Your Own Products on Amazon,"** which you can find at this link.

https://www.udemy.com/how-to-make-an-extra-1k-10k-a-month-selling-on-amazon.

Normally it retails for $199, but as a bonus for reading this book, you can get the course for $49 by using the coupon code: PENAPROMO49.

Conclusion

In conclusion, through this book, you've read a lot about many different ideas on how to make passive income. I gave you a glimpse at three of the simplest passive income business you can start, and even start making money within the next 90 days. I even shared from my personal example how I started in February of this year, and I became financially free by September

The questions I now have for you are, "What are you going to do about it now?" "When are you going to choose to be financially free?" "Are you going to let another year go by working really hard just to take home half as much money? Or are you going to make the choice to begin building the passive income you need to retire early?

You can choose to make $1,000 to $5,000 a month selling video training products on Udemy. Or you can be making $500 to $5,000 a month selling eBooks on Kindle, without doing any writing. Or you can even make $1,000 to $10,000 a month selling your own physical products on Amazon.

And there are hundreds more passive income options in the market today. The question is, "Are you ready to get started?"

Well, to help you get started, I'm going to give you a few resources to make your job easier. I have created some step-by-step trainings on Udemy to walk you through the whole process of creating passive income through: 1) creating video courses on Udemy, 2) producing Kindle Bestselling eBooks, 3) Creating your own products to sell on Amazon, and more. You can find all of these trainings at https://www.udemy.com/u/willpena/.

Normally these courses cost hundreds of dollars. But, by reading this book, you can register at a discounted price by using the promotion code—PENAPROMO49. So write that promotion code down, sign up for the videos, get more details in a step-by-step format, that I wasn't able to share in this book, and get started building passive income right away.

So, in conclusion, why passive income?

1. **More time for yourself.** You'll work only ten hours a month and make anywhere from $5,000 to $10,000 a month, minimum.

2. **More money.** You could make anywhere from $100,000 to $250,000 a year and not work that hard.

3. **More opportunities.** Financial freedom gives you the time and money to build wealth that you can't if you are working a full time schedule.

4. **More contribution.** With more time and more money, it means that you can devote more time to things that matter like your family, your church, or your community.

5. **And last, it's more fun.** It's a lot more fun to work ten hours a month than it does for working a 40 to 50 hour a week.

I hope this book has changed your life, or given you something to think about for the rest of your life.

To Your Success,
William U. Peña, MBA

Resources

Here are some additional resources to help you take the next step to creating the financially free lifestyle that you are looking for.

Udemy Selling Success Training

If you would like a more detailed and step-by-step training on making money selling video courses on Udemy, then consider my Udemy video course titled: **"How to Make $1K—$5K Selling Video Courses on Udemy,"** which you can find at this link. www.udemy.com/create-passive-income-successfully-selling-courses-on-udemy/

Sign up for this course at a discounted price by using the promotion code: PENAPROMO49.

Kindle EBook Selling Training

If you would like a more detailed and step-by-step training on making money selling eBooks on Kindle, then consider my Udemy video course titled: **"Make $500—$5000 Passively Selling EBooks on Kindle,"** which you can find at this link. https://www.udemy.com/make-passive-income-selling-kindle-ebooks.

Sign up for this course at a discounted price by using the promotion code: PENAPROMO49.

Amazon Selling System Training

If you would like a more detailed and step-by-step training on making money selling your own products on Amazon, then consider my Udemy video course titled: **"Make $1K—$10K Selling Your Own Products on Amazon,"** which you can find at this link. https://www.udemy.com/how-to-make-an-extra-1k-10k-a-month-selling-on-amazon.

Sign up for this course at a discounted price by using the promotion code: PENAPROMO49.

Other Business Training Resources by William U. Peña, MBA

If you are interested in a full list of business-training courses by William U. Peña just visit https://www.udemy.com/u/willpena/.

Other Books by William U. Peña, MBA

"Amazon Selling Secrets: How to Make $1K—$10K a Month Selling Your Own Products on Amazon."

***Get it on Amazon Kindle

Make an Extra $1K—$10K a Month in the Next 30—90 Days by Passively Selling Your Own Products on Amazon

If you are looking for an additional passive income stream, there is no better way than to tap into the 74 Billion dollar marketplace created on Amazon.

By mastering the Amazon Selling System you'll learn about in this book, you will be able to easily tap into the opportunities on Amazon, and create an additional $1K—$10K a month in passive income.

This book will teach you the step-by-step system, and highly sought after secrets of how to identify highly popular products, and then transform them into your own special brand, which customers will pay a lot of money for.

Get Your Kindle Copy Today!

"The 3 Day Entrepreneur"

***Get it on Amazon**

You Too Can Learn How to Build a 6 or 7 Figure Business Working Less Than 3 Days a Week...

What would you do if you could make more money in your business, but only work 3 days a week?

This book teaches you everything you need to know about how to live the 3 Day Entrepreneur Lifestyle, so that you can **build a 6 or 7 figure** business, but still have plenty of time to take care of the important things in your life...

...Things like your family, your kids, and your health...

It will also teach you how to free yourself to take advantage of more opportunities, like starting a new business, or building your wealth...

In this **life-changing book**, you'll hear stories from successful entrepreneurs that have decided to not only build successful businesses, but have made the time to enjoy their lifestyle, by working less.

You'll also get a **step-by-step guide** to help you experience the rewards of living the 3-Day Entrepreneur Lifestyle for yourself.

Get Your Kindle Copy Today!

Made in the USA
San Bernardino, CA
15 March 2015